KEY GEOGRAPHY

New Connections

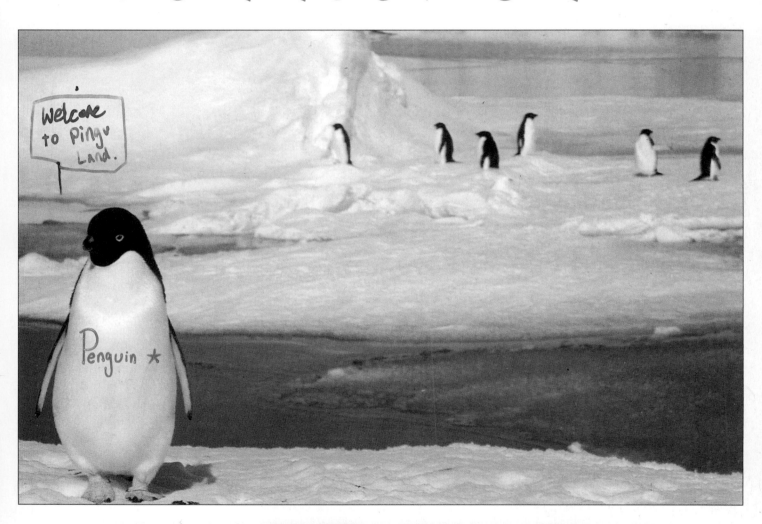

DAVID WAUGH & TONY BUSHELL

First edition published in 1992 and reprinted eight times.
Second edition published in 1997 and reprinted seven times.
This edition published in 2001 by:
Nelson Thornes Ltd
Delta Place
27 Bath Road
CHELTENHAM
GL53 7TH
United Kingdom

05 06 / 10

A catalogue record for this book is available from the British Library

First edition ISBN 0 7487 1102 3
Second edition ISBN 0 7487 2880 5
Third edition ISBN 0 7487 6074 1

Second edition designed and reset by Hilary Norman
Third edition layout by Clare Park
Illustrations by Kathy Baxendale, Nick Hawken, Malcolm Porter, Tim Smith, John Yorke, Angela Lumley, Richard Morris, Jane Cope
Cartoons by Mike Gordon
Edited by Katherine James
Photo research by Julia Hanson and Penni Bickle

Printed and bound in China by Midas Printing International Ltd.

The previous page shows Adelie penguins near Faraday Base, Antarctica

Acknowledgements

The authors and publishers are grateful to the following for permission to reproduce photographs and other copyright material in this book.

Aerofilms, pp 13, 49; Andes Press Agency, p 117; Art Directors/Trip Photography, pp 27, 30 (Farmer), 33 (Greaves), 48 left (Peters), 58 bottom (Rogers), 83 (i and iv), 102 (TSW/Click), 109 (Jelliffe); John Beatty, p 20 bottom right; Penni Bickle, p 58 top; Bradford Information Services, p 40; British Antarctic Survey, pp 54 bottom, 55 both; British Coal, p 20 bottom left; British Steel, p 35 top; Bruce Coleman, p 106; Colorific, p 62 top right; Corus, p 48 right; Countryside Commission, p 14; James Davis Travel Photography, p 101 (bottom); Greg Evans, p 101 middle; Eye Ubiquitous, pp 31 (Mowbray), 32 (Gibbons), 34 bottom right (Langfield), 44 bottom right (Wilton), 44 top right (Daniels), 50 left (Daniels), centre (Bland), right (Gill); Frank Lane Picture Agency, pp 6 top left, 26 top left, 66 bottom left, 72 bottom block - top left and bottom right; Leslie Garland, p 17; Robert Harding Picture Library, pp 6 bottom right (Gavin Heller), 11, 62 bottom right, 72 top, 88 left (Nigel Francis), 89 top (Gavin Heller); Holt Studios, p 28 bottom; The Hutchison Library, p 26 right; ICCE Photo Library, p 5 top right, 20 top left; National Power, p 60; National Rivers Authority, p 16; Panos Pictures, pp 26 bottom left; 66 bottom right; David Paterson, pp 4 top left, 6 top right, 66 top left; Pearson Education, for artwork based on diagram in The Dynamic World 1: Population, Settlement, Transport by M. J. Readman and F. M. Mayers, p99; Rochdale Libraries, p 44 top left; Rover UK, p 52; Science Photo Library, pp 28 top, 44 top right, 46 all, 66 top left, 66 top centre; Peter Smith Photography, pp 15, 97 left; Spectrum Colour Library, pp 24 left, 92 top; Tony Stone Images, pp 6 bottom left, 72 block - centre left and right; Tropix, p 93 bottom; Charles Tustian, p 20 centre right; Vauxhall Motors, p 44 bottom left; Tony Waltham - Geophotos, pp 4 top centre, top right, bottom right, 21 centre, 22 top, 24 right, 97 right; Simon Warner, pp 21 top and bottom, 66 top right; Judith Waugh, p 85 right; The Wildlife Trusts, p 82; Mike Williams, pp 29.

Extract from OS Landranger 128 reproduced with the permission of the Controller of Her Majesty's Stationery Office © Crown Copyright; Licence 07000U (p53).

All other photos were supplied by the authors.

Every effort has been made to contact copyright holders and we apologise if any have been overlooked.

Contents

1 Weathering, rivers and coasts   *4*

2 Primary activities   *24*

3 Secondary activities   *44*

4 Environmental concerns   *66*

5 Population   *84*

6 Kenya, a developing country   *100*

Glossary   *118*

What is weathering?

There is a great variety of different scenery in the world. Some places are mountainous, some are flat, some can be described as spectacular and others simply as interesting. Geographers call the scenery of a place the **landscape**. Some examples of the world's landscapes are shown in photos **A**, **B** and **C**.

The surface of the earth and the landscapes we see around us not only differ from place to place, but they are changing all the time.

Rain, sun, wind and frost constantly break down the rocks. Great mountain ranges get worn down, valleys are made wider and deeper, and coastlines are changed. The breaking up of the earth's surface in this way is due to **weathering** and **erosion**. Weathering takes place when the rocks are attacked by the weather. Erosion is the wearing away of the land. These two pages show some examples of weathering. Erosion is explained more fully on pages 6 and 7.

A Mount Everest

B Monument Valley, USA

C Guilin, China

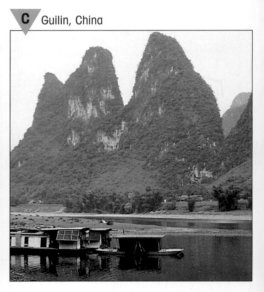

Freeze–thaw weathering

This can also be called frost shattering. Water may get into a crack in a rock and freeze. As the water turns to ice it expands and causes the crack to open a little. When it thaws the ice melts and changes back to water. Repeated freezing and thawing weakens the rock and splits it into jagged pieces. This type of weathering is common in mountainous areas where temperatures are often around freezing point.

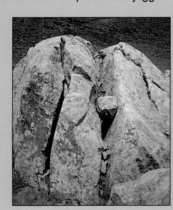

Water fills a crack in a rock

The water freezes and the crack is made wider

The rock breaks into several pieces

Onion-skin weathering

This happens when a rock is repeatedly heated and cooled. As it is heated, the outer layer of the rock expands slightly and as it cools the rock contracts. Continual expansion and contraction causes small pieces of the rock surface to peel off like the skin of an onion. This type of weathering is common in desert areas where it is very hot during the day but cool at night.

Biological weathering

This is due to the action of plants and animals. Seeds may fall into cracks in the rocks where shelter and moisture help them grow into small plants or trees. As the roots develop they gradually force the cracks to widen and the rock to fall apart. Eventually whole rocks can be broken into small pieces. Burrowing animals such as rabbits, moles and even earthworms can also help break down rock.

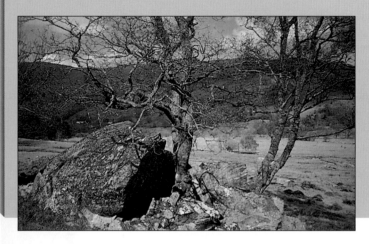

Chemical weathering

This is caused by the action of water. Ordinary rainwater contains small amounts of acid. When it comes into contact with rock the acid attacks it and causes the rock to rot and crumble away. The results of this can be seen on buildings and in churchyards where the stone has been worn away or pitted. Water and heat make chemical weathering happen faster, so it is greatest in places that are warm and wet.

Activities

1 Make a larger copy of diagram **D**.
   a) Write in the meaning of weathering.
   b) Add labels to the weathering features.

Weathering is ____

2 Copy and complete these sentences.
   a) Freeze–thaw weathering is . . .
   b) Onion-skin weathering is . . .
   c) Chemical weathering is . . .

3 With the help of a labelled diagram show how freeze–thaw weathering can break up rocks.

4 a) Make a larger copy of diagram **E**.
   b) Show how root action can break up rocks, by adding the following labels to the correct boxes. Give your diagram a title.

Roots develop

Roots break up rocks

Crack gives moisture and shelter

Tree grows

Seeds blow into crack

E

E X T R A

Draw these simple sketches of photos **A**, **B** and **C**. Give each sketch a title and underneath say what type of weathering is likely to be most important there. Give reasons for your answers.

Summary

Weathering is the breakdown of rocks by water, frost and temperature change. Rocks can also be broken down by the effects of plants and animals.

What is erosion . . .

Weathering and erosion work together. Weathering breaks up and weakens the surface of rocks while erosion wears away and removes the loosened material. The action of rivers, the sea, ice and wind are the chief types of erosion. Human erosion is also important. Bulldozers and lorries can dig out and move large amounts of soil and loose rock, so changing the landscape. People also remove trees and vegetation which can allow water, wind and ice to erode land more easily.

The work of rivers, the sea, ice and wind are explained in **A** below.

A

Rivers

Every day rivers wear away tiny bits of rock from their bed, and eat into the banks on either side of the channel. This material is carried downstream and deposited when the water slows down. In times of flood large boulders may be loosened and rolled down the river bed.

Ice

A **glacier** is a tongue of ice moving down a valley. Stones and boulders that fall on to it freeze into the ice and act like sandpaper on the rocks beneath. As the glacier moves, it carries the material downwards and at the same time wears away the valley bottom and sides.

Sea

Coastlines are under constant attack by **waves**. During storms each wave hits the rock with a weight of several tonnes. When this is repeated many times, the rock is weakened and pieces break off. **Currents** carry loose material away and deposit it elsewhere.

Wind

Explorers who cross deserts in cars often find their paintwork worn away and their windscreens scratched. This is because the wind picks up tiny particles of sand and blasts them against anything that is in the way. Rocks in desert areas are often eroded into strange shapes by this sand-blasting effect.

... and how can it help shape the land?

Look at cartoon **B** on the right. It shows some gardeners who are trying to alter a garden by digging out soil (erosion), moving it in a wheelbarrow (transportation), and dumping it somewhere else (deposition). The more energy they have, the more soil they can dig or transport. When they are tired the digging slows down and they lack the strength to push the barrow, resulting in it toppling over and dumping its load.

On a larger scale, mountains, valleys, plains and coasts are shaped and changed by water, ice and wind. **Erosion** wears away the land, **transportation** moves the material from one place to another, and **deposition** builds up new landforms.

B

EROSION... ➡ TRANSPORTATION ➡ DEPOSITION

Activities

1 a) List the following in order of how hard they are. Give the hardest first and the softest last.

| steel | chalk | soap | wood |

| rubber | diamond | plastic |

b) Put a line under the two you think would be the most difficult to wear down.

c) Choose any three from your list and say how they might be worn down.

2 Of the five statements below, three are correct. Write out the correct ones.
- Weathering is the breakdown of rock by nature.
- Erosion is the wearing away of rock.
- Weathering and erosion are the same.
- Weathering moves material from one place to another.
- Erosion includes the removal of loose material.

3 a) Make a large copy of table **C**.
  b) Add labels to each drawing.
  c) Write a short description for each type of erosion.

EXTRA

Cartoon **B** shows erosion, transportation and deposition in a garden. How else could this be shown? What about a bulldozer, washing dishes or sandpapering wood? For one of these ideas, or for one of your own, draw a simple labelled cartoon to show how it works.

C Types of erosion

Type	Description

Summary Erosion is the wearing away of rock and its removal by streams, ice, waves and wind. Erosion, transportation and deposition help shape the land.

How do rivers shape the land?

Rivers work hard. They hardly stop and they continually erode and move material downstream. They are a major force in shaping and altering the land. Running water by itself actually has little power to wear away rocks. What happens is that the water pushes boulders, stones and rock particles along the river's course. As it does so, the loose material scrapes the river bed and banks and loosens other material. Much of what is worn away is then transported by the river and put down somewhere else. In this way rivers can wear out and deepen valleys. They can also change their shape by depositing material.

The landforms to be seen along a river change as it flows from source to mouth. These two pages explain the features of a river in its upper course which is usually in the hills or mountains. Diagram **A** and photo **B** show how a river cuts out a steep-sided valley that is V-shaped.

A

Eroding down

Weathering

Slope transport

V-shaped valley

1 The river erodes downwards as boulders, stones and rock particles are bounced and scraped along the channel bed.

2 As the river cuts down, the steep sides are attacked by weathering. This breaks up and loosens the soil and rock.

3 The loosened material slowly creeps down the slope because of gravity or is washed into the river by rainwater. The river carries it away.

4 The end result is a steep-sided valley that has the shape of a letter 'V'.

B

The making of a V-shaped valley

Slopes attacked by weathering

River erodes downwards

Gravity and rainwater move material downwards (slope transport)

River source

V-shaped valley

Rocks and pebbles moved along the bed

Weathered and eroded material transported by river

Table **C** below and sketch **D** give some features of a river and its valley.

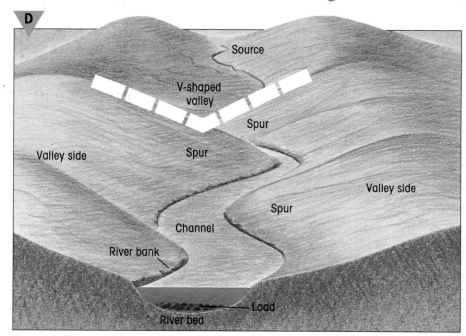

Source	Where a river starts
Spurs	Ridges of land around which a river winds
Valley sides	The slopes on either side of a river
V-shaped valley	The shape of a valley in its upper course
Channel	The course of a river
River banks	The sides of a river channel
River bed	The bottom of a river channel
Load	Material that is carried or moved by the river

Activities

1 Describe how rivers erode their channels. Include these words in your description:

`pushes` `scrapes` `loosens` `moves` `drops`

2 **a)** Make a large copy of diagram **E**.
   b) Show how a valley gets to be V-shaped by describing what happens at ①, ②, ③ and ④.
   c) Give your diagram a suitable title.

3 **a)** Sketch **F** is a simplified drawing of the river valley shown in photo **B**. Make a copy of the sketch.
   b) Add the terms below to your sketch in the correct places. The information at the top of this page will help you.

`river channel` `river bank` `load`

`valley side` `spur` `V-shaped valley`

Summary

Rivers erode, transport and deposit material. This helps shape the land. V-shaped valleys are a common feature of a river in its upper course.

A

979 m
Angel Falls

244 m

Canary
Wharf
Tower

50 m
Niagara Falls

High Force ——— 20 m

What causes waterfalls?

Waterfalls are an attractive and often spectacular feature of a river. The highest waterfall in the world is the Angel Falls in South America. Its total height is 979 metres. That is about four times the height of Britain's tallest building, the Canary Wharf Tower in London's Docklands. Waterfalls in Britain are much smaller than this (diagram **A**). One of the finest is High Force in the north of England. It has a height of just 20 metres. It is most impressive in times of flood.

Probably the best known waterfall in the world is Niagara Falls. It lies on the Niagara River which forms part of the border between Canada and the United States. In this area, a band of hard limestone rock lies on top of softer shales and sandstone. The river flows over the top of the hard rock then plunges down a 50 metre cliff. At the bottom of the cliff the water has worn away the softer rocks to form a pool over 50 metres deep. This is called a **plunge pool**. Down from the falls is the Niagara Gorge. A **gorge** is a valley with almost vertical sides that has been carved out by the river and the waterfall. Photo **D** shows the gorge and waterfall at Niagara.

Sketch **B** shows the Niagara Falls area. The falls here are eating into the cliffs behind the waterfall at nearly one metre a year. The gorge that has been left behind is now 11 kilometres long.

Many waterfalls are formed in the same way as Niagara. They occur when rivers flow over different types of rock. The soft rock wears away faster than the hard rock. In time a step develops over which the river plunges as a waterfall. Water also cuts away rock behind the waterfall. This causes the falls to move back and leave a gorge as it goes. Diagram **C** shows how a waterfall may be worn away by a river.

B

Lake Erie

CANADA

Niagara River

Goat Island

Horseshoe Falls

UNITED STATES OF AMERICA

American Falls

Original position of falls

Niagara Gorge

11 km

CANADA

Hard rock
Soft rock

N

C

River

Hard rock

Soft rock

Plunge pool

Waterfall moves back

1 Falling water and rock particles or boulders loosen and wear away the softer rock.

2 The hard rock above is undercut as erosion of the soft rock continues.

3 The hard rock collapses into the plunge pool to be broken up and washed away by the river. The position of the falls moves back.

4 Erosion continues and the waterfall slowly eats its way upstream, leaving a gorge behind.

Activities

1 Map **E** shows the Niagara Falls area.
  a) Make an accurate copy of the map.
  b) Colour the water blue and the land area green.
  c) Label the following:

| USA | Canada | American Falls | Niagara River |

| Horseshoe Falls | Niagara Gorge | Goat Island |

  d) Draw on and label the original position of the falls.
  e) The falls have taken 30,000 years to wear back 11 km. Draw on and label where the falls might be 10,000 years from now.

2 a) Make a larger copy of diagram **F**.
  b) Put these labels in the correct places.

| Hard rock | Soft rock | Plunge pool |

| Hard rock breaks off | Eroded material |

| Undercutting | Waterfall moves back |

3 Sort the phrases in **G** into the correct order and link them with arrows to show how a waterfall may be worn away by a river.

Summary

Many waterfalls are a result of water wearing away soft rock more quickly than hard rock. As a waterfall erodes back, a gorge may be produced.

11

What happens on a river bend?

Have you noticed that rivers rarely flow in a straight line? Usually they twist and turn as they make their way down to the sea. The only time they are straight seems to be when people interfere with them by building banks or diverting their course.

Bends develop on a river mainly because of the water's eroding power. Think about when you are a passenger in a car and it goes around a corner. You are thrown towards the outside of the curve, often with quite a lot of force. The same happens when a river goes around a bend. The force of the water is greatest towards the outside of the bend. When it hits the bank it causes erosion. This erosion deepens the channel at that point and wears away the bank to make a small **river cliff**. On the inside of the bend, water movement is slower. Material builds up here due to deposition. This makes the bank gently sloping and the river channel shallow.

Diagram **A** shows what happens on a river bend. At the bottom of the diagram is a **cross-section**. This shows what the river would look like if a slice was cut across it from one side to the other.

 A

Water flows downstream

Slowest flow is on the inside of the bend

Fastest flow is on the outside of the bend

Deposition takes place

Erosion takes place

A small beach of material builds up

The bank is worn away and a river cliff develops

The channel is shallow

The channel is deepened

B
Deposition on the inside of a river bend

C
Erosion on the outside of a river bend

Look at sketch **D** and photo **E**. The river has many bends. These are called **meanders** and are a common feature of most rivers. On either side of the river channel there is an area of flat land called the **flood plain**. This area gets covered in water when the river overflows its banks. Flood plains are made up of **alluvium**, a fine muddy material that is left behind after floods. Alluvium is sometimes called **silt**.

Flood plains are useful to people because they are areas of flat land and have rich fertile soil. This makes them good for building on and for farming.

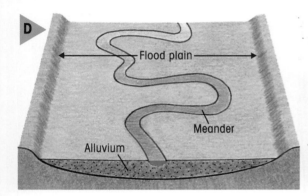

Flood plain

Meander

Alluvium

Activities

1 Look at diagram **F**, which is a simple cross-section of a river bend.
   a) Draw the cross-section.
   b) Write the labels from **G** in the correct places.
   c) Give your drawing a title.
   d) Describe why one side of the river bend is different from the other.

2 **a)** Make simple sketches of photos **B** and **C**.
   b) For each sketch describe the river feature that it shows.
   c) Explain how each feature was made.

3 Give the meaning of the terms shown in sketch **D**.

F

G

Slowest flow   Erosion   Gentle slope
Deep water   Deposition
River cliff   Fastest flow   Shallow water

E X T R A S

1 Write down two reasons why the flood plain of a valley is good for farming.

2 Give one problem of farming the flood plain. Suggest what could be done to reduce the problem.

Summary

A river's course is seldom straight. It usually has many bends which cause it to meander down its valley. The outside of a river bend is worn away by erosion while the inside is built up by deposition.

How does the sea shape the coast?

The sea is never still. On quiet days the movement is slow and gentle, and the sea is flat and almost calm. On stormy days large waves crash against the shore. These large waves have such force that they can drive a ship against the rocks or smash up sea defences and piers. The sea can also wear away the coast and move bits of rock and sand from one place to another. This ability to erode, transport and deposit material produces many interesting coastal landforms.

Erosion landforms are made by the wearing away of the coast (photo **A**). In stormy conditions the sea picks up loose rocks and throws them at the shore. This bombardment undercuts cliffs, opens up cracks and breaks up loose rocks into smaller and smaller pieces. Areas which have soft rocks are worn away more easily than those with hard rocks. The soft rock areas become **bays** and the hard rock areas become **headlands**. A bay is an opening in the coastline. A headland is a stretch of land jutting out into the sea.

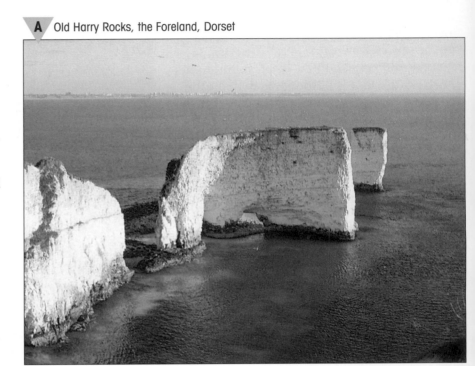

A Old Harry Rocks, the Foreland, Dorset

Sketch **B** shows how a headland is eroded by the sea and how other landforms develop.

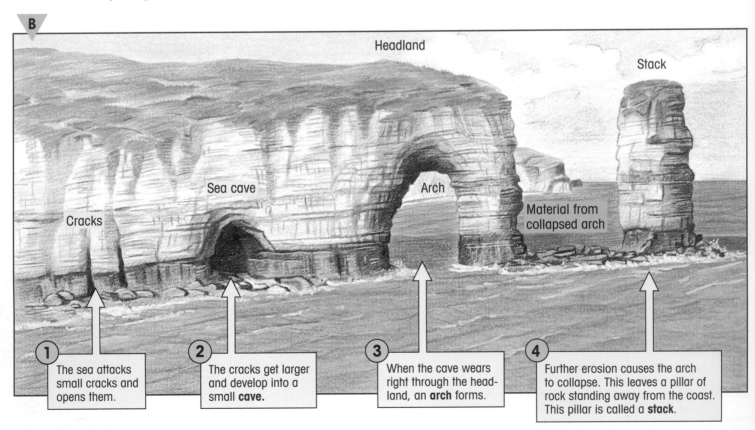

B

Headland

Stack

Sea cave

Arch

Cracks

Material from collapsed arch

① The sea attacks small cracks and opens them.

② The cracks get larger and develop into a small **cave.**

③ When the cave wears right through the head-land, an **arch** forms.

④ Further erosion causes the arch to collapse. This leaves a pillar of rock standing away from the coast. This pillar is called a **stack**.

Beaches are one of the most common features of our shoreline. They are formed when material worn away from one part of the coast is carried along and dropped somewhere else. A beach is an example of a **deposition landform**. A **spit** is a special type of beach extending out into the sea. It is a long finger of sand and shingle that often grows out across a bay or the mouth of a river.

Photo **C** and map **D** show Spurn Head spit. It is 6 kilometres long and forms a sweeping curve that stretches halfway across the mouth of the River Humber. It is continually changing its shape as new material is deposited and old material is worn away or moved elsewhere.

C

The making of Spurn Head spit

1 Erosion of coastline north of Spurn Head

2 Eroded material transported down the coast by sea currents

3 Material dropped where coastline changes direction

4 Spit grows out from coast as more material builds up

5 End of spit curved by action of the waves.

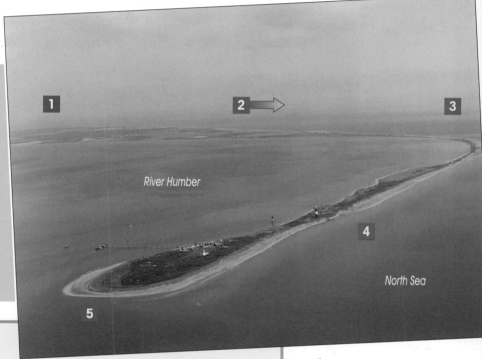

Activities

1 **a)** Make a sketch of photo **A**.
   b) Mark and label on your sketch the following terms:

   | crack | cave | arch | stack |

   | material from a collapsed arch |

   c) Give your sketch a title.

2 **a)** Copy map **D** showing the Spurn Head area.
   b) Shade **orange** the area of coastal erosion from Flamborough Head to the northern end of Spurn Head.
   c) Shade **purple** the areas of deposition on Spurn Head and in the mouth of the Humber.
   d) Draw an arrow to show the movement of eroded material along the coast.

3 **a)** Explain why some of the villages on map **D** have been 'lost'.
   b) How has the shape of the mouth of the Humber changed since Roman times?

D

Key
- – – – Coastline in Roman times
- • Lost village or town
- Erosion
- Deposition

4 Explain how the spit at Spurn Head has been made. Include these terms in your writing.
   erosion • Flamborough Head • transportation • currents • deposition • Spurn Head • grows • 6 km

Summary

The coastline is always changing its shape. Some parts are being worn away by erosion while other parts are being built up by deposition.

How are rivers polluted?

Water is one of the basic needs of human life and for this reason rivers have long been good places to locate towns and cities. Rivers can provide water for domestic use and supply the needs of industry and agriculture. They may also be used for communications, for the generation of power and, more recently, for recreational purposes. Sadly, they are also used for the disposal of unwanted waste. Waste that is put into rivers from farmland or from cities is continually carried away but there is a limit to how much a river can get rid of. When the limit is reached there is a serious **pollution** problem.

The River Tyne is an example of a polluted river. Most of its pollution comes from the large industrial towns of Newcastle upon Tyne and Gateshead. As map **A** shows, raw sewage from nearly a million people as well as waste from scores of factories was dumped directly into the river. The result was unpleasant sights and smells, danger to public health from poisons in the water, and a biologically dead river that was unable to support fish or any other sort of life.

A

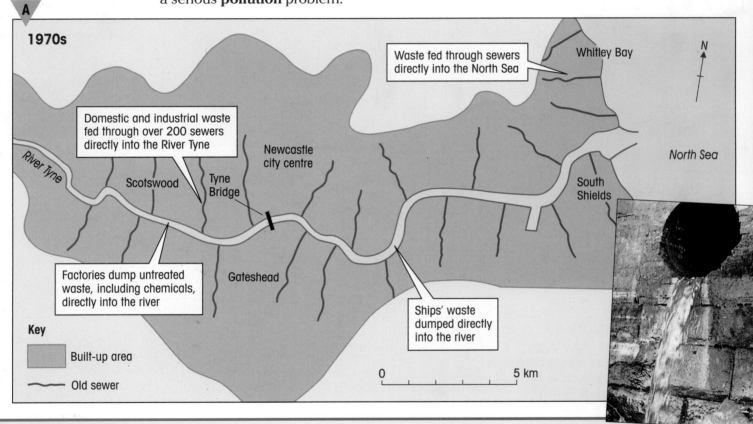

1970s

Waste fed through sewers directly into the North Sea

Whitley Bay

N

Domestic and industrial waste fed through over 200 sewers directly into the River Tyne

Newcastle city centre

North Sea

River Tyne

Scotswood

Tyne Bridge

South Shields

Factories dump untreated waste, including chemicals, directly into the river

Gateshead

Ships' waste dumped directly into the river

Key

Built-up area

Old sewer

0   5 km

Activities

WARNING

1 Give **six** reasons why many towns and cities are located beside rivers.

2 Draw a warning poster to be placed along the banks of the Tyne showing the dangers of pollution in the 1970s. Your poster should show the facts, be colourful and attract attention.

3 Imagine that you work for a pollution research unit. Write a short report to the National Rivers Authority giving the main causes of pollution on the River Tyne. Use the headings *Domestic*, *Industrial* and *Shipping* for your report. Make your report about a page long.

4 Describe the River Tyne clean-up scheme by writing out the following in the correct order. Start with 'Domestic waste . . .' and end with '. . . and fish return.'

And how can they be cleaned up?

On a hot day in the summer of 1969 a Council meeting held near the River Tyne had to be stopped because the smell from the river was so bad. The river today is very different. It is clean, attractive and an ideal place for water sports like sailing, rowing, powerboat racing and windsurfing. It is also reckoned to be one of the best salmon fishing rivers in England.

This dramatic improvement has been brought about in two main ways:
- first, by stopping industry from dumping waste directly into the river
- second, by setting up a huge £150 million

clean-up scheme involving the construction of 73 km of new sewers. The scheme is explained in map **C**.

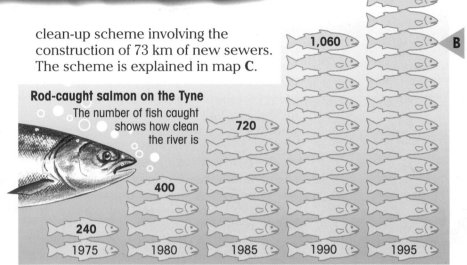

Rod-caught salmon on the Tyne
The number of fish caught shows how clean the river is

1975	1980	1985	1990	1995
240	400	720	1,060	1,380

B

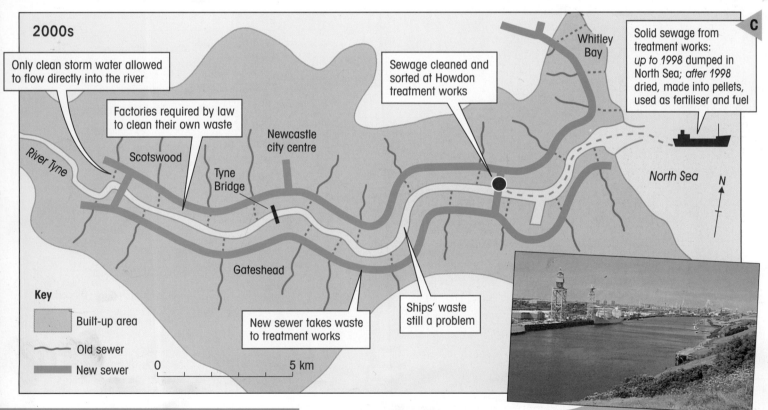

2000s

Only clean storm water allowed to flow directly into the river

Factories required by law to clean their own waste

Sewage cleaned and sorted at Howdon treatment works

Whitley Bay

Solid sewage from treatment works: *up to 1998* dumped in North Sea; *after 1998* dried, made into pellets, used as fertiliser and fuel

C

River Tyne

Scotswood

Newcastle city centre

Tyne Bridge

Gateshead

North Sea

N

New sewer takes waste to treatment works

Ships' waste still a problem

Key
- Built-up area
- Old sewer
- New sewer

0 ___ 5 km

Add a title to your completed description.
- Domestic waste from houses
- Clean water is returned to the river
- flows down the new sewer to
- so the river quality improves
- goes into the sewers then
- the treatment works.
- and fish return.

E X T R A

For a polluted stream, river or lake that you know:
- Say what the pollution problem is.
- Describe the causes of pollution.
- Suggest how the pollution problem may be reduced.

Summary

Rivers can be very useful to people but their misuse may lead to pollution. Clean-up schemes and regulations to control waste disposal are needed to reduce river pollution.

The North Sea — Europe's dustbin?

The North Sea is very important. Over 50 million people live close to its shores and no other sea in the world has so much industry operating around it. The sea is a great provider. It gives us sand and gravel for the building industry, cooling water for power stations and fish for food. Coal, oil and gas are extracted from below its shallow, stormy waters and busy shipping routes criss-cross the sea from one side to the other. The sea is also important for recreation – a place to sail on, swim in, or simply a place to relax beside.

Unfortunately the North Sea is also filthy. In fact, it is one of the dirtiest and most polluted of all the seas in the world. It has been called 'Europe's dustbin' because everyone dumps their unwanted rubbish into it. It is estimated that over one billion tonnes of pollution enter the sea every year. Poisonous chemicals, domestic sewage, oil, litter and even radioactive waste all get dumped into the sea.

Some of the causes and effects of this pollution are shown in map **A** below.

A

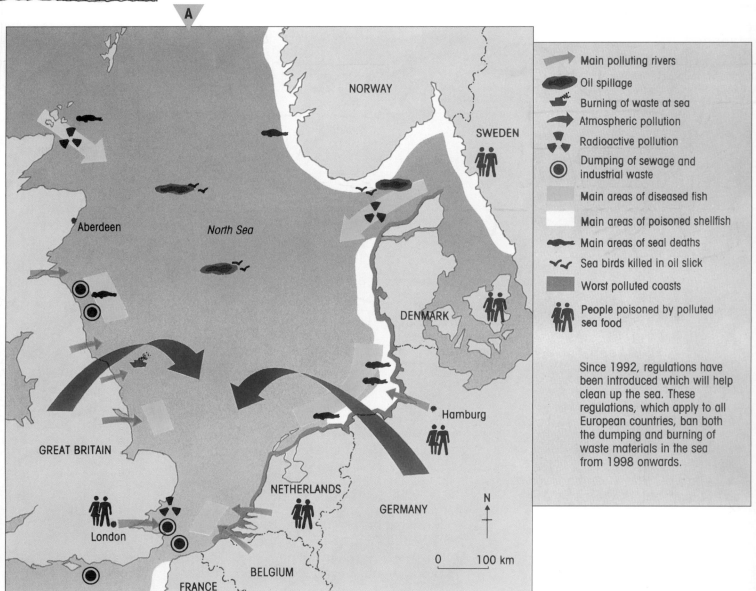

Legend:
- Main polluting rivers
- Oil spillage
- Burning of waste at sea
- Atmospheric pollution
- Radioactive pollution
- Dumping of sewage and industrial waste
- Main areas of diseased fish
- Main areas of poisoned shellfish
- Main areas of seal deaths
- Sea birds killed in oil slick
- Worst polluted coasts
- People poisoned by polluted sea food

Since 1992, regulations have been introduced which will help clean up the sea. These regulations, which apply to all European countries, ban both the dumping and burning of waste materials in the sea from 1998 onwards.

Cleaning up the North Sea is very difficult. We do not know exactly what is dumped in the sea or what actual damage it does. Nor do we know how to clean up the sea or stop people dirtying it. Eight different countries border the North Sea and each blames the other for being the worst polluter. How can laws be made which will be accepted by all? Cleaning up a mess is never easy but unless something is done soon, the damage to the sea will be so great that it may never recover.

Look at diagram **B**. It shows some of the solutions and problems of cleaning up the North Sea.

Activities

1 **a)** Name the countries that have coastlines on the North Sea.
   b) Which countries suffer the worst coastal pollution?

2 Draw table **C** below, and complete it by writing in six causes and six effects of North Sea pollution.
   Note – there is no need to link each cause with an effect.

North Sea pollution	
Causes	Effects

3 A ship has to take some cargo from Aberdeen down the east coast of Britain to London. From there it has to sail across to Hamburg in Germany. Follow the ship's route on map **A** and list the types of pollution it will pass through.

4 Give six reasons why it is difficult to clean up the North Sea.

EXTRAS

1 Imagine that you are taking part in a march against North Sea pollution.
   - Design a banner to take with you.
   - On the banner give suggestions as to how the sea might be cleaned up.
   - Add drawings and colour to make your banner interesting and attractive.

2 Draw the flags from diagram **B** and match each one to a North Sea country.

Summary

The North Sea is badly polluted. Pollution comes from rivers, coastal discharges, the air and dumping at sea. Solving the problem of pollution is difficult and needs the joint efforts of many countries.

The river enquiry

The Pennine Way is one of Britain's best known long distance walks. It stretches some 410 km (256 miles) from the Derbyshire Peak District northwards to the Cheviots and into Scotland. One of the walk's most interesting sections is in Upper Teesdale. Here the trail follows the River Tees through some wild and impressive scenery. At one point it overlooks High Force, one of Britain's finest waterfalls.

Every year the Upper Teesdale area receives more and more visitors. Some people have suggested that a small pamphlet explaining the features of the area would be helpful. This would enable walkers and tourists to understand their surroundings and help them enjoy their stay in the area. Your task is to produce the pamphlet by answering the enquiry question below.

To do this you will need to describe the main features of the area and find out how they were formed. You could work by yourself, with a partner or even in a small group. You might be able to use a computer to word process your work and make it look more professional. Pages 6 to 13 of this book will be helpful to you.

How does the River Tees shape the land?

Your aims for this piece of work are:
- to answer the enquiry question
- to produce an information pamphlet for use by walkers and other visitors to Upper Teesdale
- to describe and explain the main physical features of the area
- to make your pamphlet attractive, interesting, helpful and simple to understand.

The Pennine Way

1 Introduction – what is the area like, and how can rivers shape the land?

You will need to use maps and writing here. Diagrams and even cartoons might also help.

a) First say what the Pennine Way is and show where it is located.

b) Next describe Upper Teesdale. You will need to:
- say whereabouts it is
- describe the scenery
- suggest why it is a popular area for visitors.

The text and map on page 20 and the sketch below will help you with this. Try to use the words on the notice board in your description.

c) Finally, describe how rivers can shape the land through erosion, transportation and deposition processes.

UPPER TEESDALE
highland area. wild. moorland. valley. rural. beautiful. waterfall. Pennine Way. High Force. scattered farms. gorge.

• 544
Cronkley Scar
A
B
Saur Hill Bridge
Pennine Way
River Tees
Cronkley Bridge
B 6277
• 412
• 414
High Force
Gorge
C
Hotel

Key
- – – – Pennine Way
- ◄Ⓐ Photo location
- —— Main road
- •414 Height in metres

→ N

21

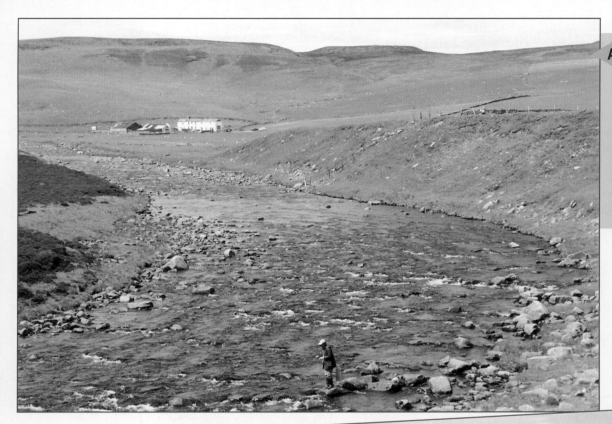

The river on this bend is about 25 metres wide with a depth of no more than half a metre. The deepest water is on the right of the photo.

2 What are the main landform features and how were they formed?

a) Look carefully at photos **A**, **B** and **C**, which show a river bend, an area that floods, and High Force waterfall and gorge.

b) For each one in turn describe the feature and explain the river processes that helped form it. You could use labelled sketches, cross-section drawings, block diagrams and writing here.

Try to present your work in a clear and interesting way. It is important that your readers find your work attractive and are able to understand fully what you are showing them.

B

At times of flood, the river here is almost 300 metres wide. The valley floor is made up of alluvium (silt) and boulders of all sizes.

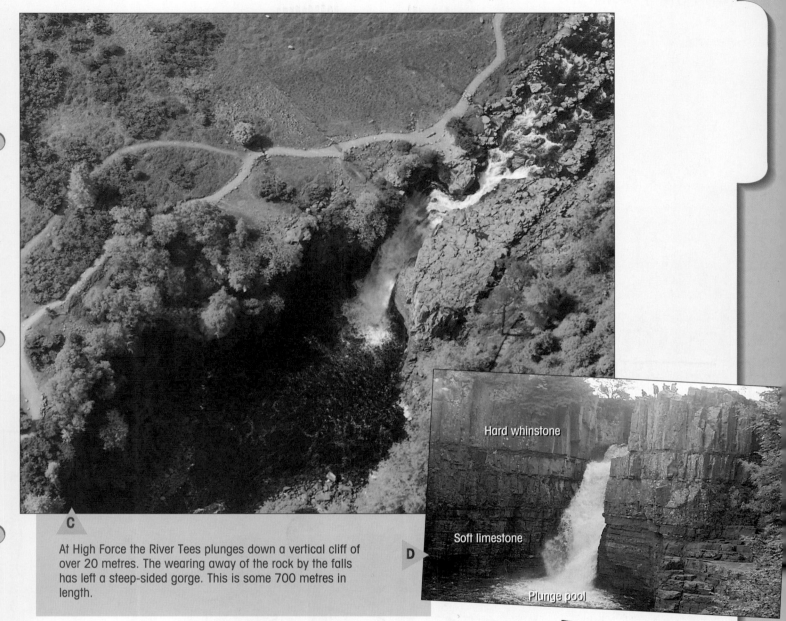

C

At High Force the River Tees plunges down a vertical cliff of over 20 metres. The wearing away of the rock by the falls has left a steep-sided gorge. This is some 700 metres in length.

D

Hard whinstone

Soft limestone

Plunge pool

3 Conclusion

This should be a summary to go at the end of your information pamphlet. There could be two parts to it. Together they should answer the question set by the enquiry question.

a) First you need to describe briefly the three main landform features of the area, and show their location. You could do this by adding labels to a map or sketch like the one on page 21. You should write no more than about 20 words for each label.

b) Secondly you should write a paragraph to explain how the River Tees has helped shape the land in this area.

What are primary industries?

Economic activities are ways by which people can earn their living. One of these groups of economic activity is called **primary industry**. Primary industry is when people collect and use **natural resources**. These natural resources are sometimes called **raw materials**. We get raw materials from the natural (physical) environment of the earth and the sea. There are four main types of primary industry. They are shown on photos **A**, **B**, **C** and **D**.

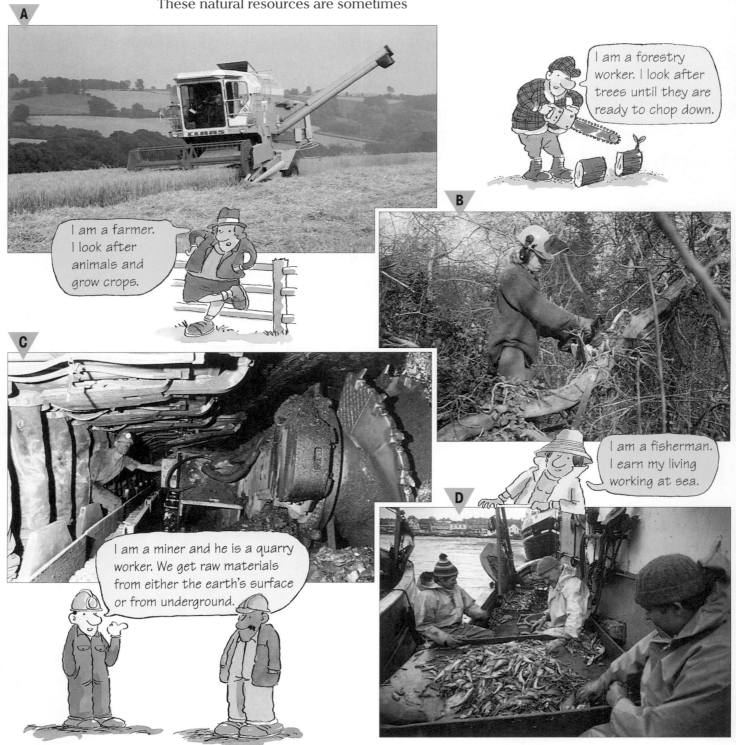

A

I am a farmer. I look after animals and grow crops.

I am a forestry worker. I look after trees until they are ready to chop down.

B

C

I am a miner and he is a quarry worker. We get raw materials from either the earth's surface or from underground.

I am a fisherman. I earn my living working at sea.

D

How can collecting natural resources harm the environment?

The **mining** of coal, the **quarrying** of slate and the collection of gravel all provide jobs for local people and earn money for the country. However, the collection of natural resources from the ground has bad points as well as good points. Photo **E** is a quarry in a National Park. It has been labelled to show some of the bad effects it has upon the landscape, the local people and the wildlife.

Photo **F** shows an old gravel quarry. Gravel is used in the building industry. Photo **G** shows a coal **spoil tip**. Sometimes when a useful natural resource is collected so too is material for which we have no use. This waste material has to be dumped and forms spoil tips.

Loose rock can be dangerous

Loss of farmland

Noise and vibrations from blasting affects wildlife and buildings

Dust from blasting causes air pollution

E

Loss of grass and trees where wildlife used to live

Heavy lorries cause noise and air pollution and can make narrow country roads dangerous

Ugly buildings spoil the scenery

Activities

1 What do we mean by a 'primary industry'?

2 Which of the following jobs are primary activities?

| sheep farmer | doctor | coal miner |
| shopkeeper | lorry driver | forestry worker |

3 Copy table **H** below. Complete it with the help of photo **E**. Your completed table should show how quarrying can harm the landscape and affect people and wildlife.

H

Harmful effects of quarrying on:		
Landscape	People	Wildlife

F

G

For either photo **F**, photo **G** or an example in your home area, give **three** ways by which mining or collecting gravel can affect the landscape, people and wildlife.

E X T R A

Summary

Primary industries are when people collect and use natural resources. The collecting of natural resources can harm the landscape and affect people and wildlife.

25

How can damaged environments be improved?

Old quarries, spoil tips and gravel tips are not very attractive. They can also be very dangerous. As our interest in the environment grows, more attempts are being made to improve these unsightly areas and if possible make them useful again.

Photo **A** shows an old gravel pit that has been improved. The ground has been made safe, the water cleaned and the lake converted into a water sports area. Other gravel pits in Britain have been turned into nature reserves.

Spoil tips result from mining and quarrying. In 1966 one tip at Aberfan in South Wales became so wet after heavy rain that it flowed downhill. It covered a primary school and some cottages. Of the 147 people killed, 116 were children. Since then the steep sides of many spoil tips have been made more gentle and have been planted with trees and grass (diagram **B**).

Quarries are often found in National Parks and other attractive areas of countryside. Quarries have now to be landscaped and screened while they are being used (sketch **C**). When quarrying is finished, the land has to be restored to its original appearance. This can be very expensive. It may also be difficult to get plants to grow as quarries are often short of water and soil. Sketch **D** shows a method used in the Lake District. The quarry is filled with household waste, the ground is made level, topsoil is added and then trees are planted.

B

Original spoil tip
Steep sides
No vegetation

New 'spoil tip' with gentle sides
Grass and trees planted to stop the tip moving and to make it more attractive

C

Quarry does not cut into skyline

Only cuts into part of the hillside

Is screened by trees and shrubs

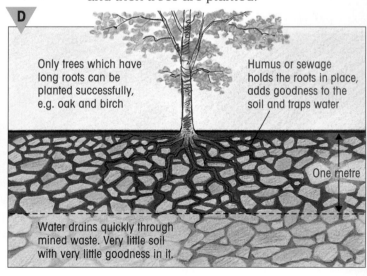

D

Only trees which have long roots can be planted successfully, e.g. oak and birch

Humus or sewage holds the roots in place, adds goodness to the soil and traps water

One metre

Water drains quickly through mined waste. Very little soil with very little goodness in it.

Sketch **F** shows a restored quarry near the Roman Wall in Northumberland National Park. The quarry was used until 1978. When it closed it left a hole 30 metres deep and the size of 16 hockey or football pitches. The hole was flooded and was dangerous. The quarry also had many old, unused buildings and piles of mined waste.

Some of the ways in which the quarry has been improved since then are shown on sketch **F**. Photo **E** shows how far the improvements had got by 1997.

Roman Wall (Hadrian's Wall)

Bare rock

Grass and trees planted

Dangerous steep slope reduced by moving soil

Quarry screened from road by fully grown trees

Grass and trees planted on old mineral waste

Rock outcrop

Shallow lake cleared of rubbish

Wet areas drained

Trees planted

Toilet block made from local stone

Picnic area and possible nature reserve

Small car park

ROME RULES OK!

It's changed a lot since I was last here!

Activities

1 Choose **either** a gravel pit **or** a spoil tip. It can either be one of those shown on page 26 or one near to where you live.
   a) Say if it is a gravel pit or a spoil tip.
   b) Explain how it used to spoil the scenery and was dangerous to people.
   c) Describe how it has been made more attractive and less dangerous.

2 Look at sketch **F** and photo **E**.
   a) In 1978 a 'Warning – keep out' notice was put up in the quarry. Draw the notice and add what might have been written on it.
   b) How had the changes made to the quarry by 1997 improved the landscape for
   ● people
   ● wildlife?

3 You and your family decide to visit the quarry for a half a day. Describe what each member of your family might do during your visit.

WARNING KEEP OUT

Summary

Attempts are now being made to improve landscapes which have been damaged by mining and quarrying. These improvements may cost a lot of money and take a long time.

What types of farming are there in Britain?

Farming, or **agriculture**, is the way that people produce food by growing crops and raising animals. There are three main types of farming in Britain.

- **Arable** is the ploughing of land and the growing of crops.
- **Pastoral** is leaving the land under grass for the grazing of animals.
- **Mixed farming** is when crops are grown and animals are reared in the same area.

Farming, especially in Britain, is big business. Farmers must carefully choose the best type of farming for the place where they farm. Deciding which is the best type depends upon several physical and human factors.

- **Physical factors** are climate, relief and soils.
- **Human factors** include farm size, technology, machinery, distance from markets, and transport.

A Arable farming

I grow crops like wheat, barley, potatoes and carrots. They need flat land with deep, fertile soil and a warm climate. There must be some rain, but not too much. Sunshine helps the crops to ripen. Modern machinery helps us with our work. We use it to plough the land and harvest crops.

Arable farmers who grow crops that are heavy to transport (such as potatoes) or soon go bad (such as strawberries) must be near to the market.

B Hill sheep farming

On our farm we make a living by selling wool, lamb and mutton at the local market. We live in the hills but sheep are very tough and can graze land that is too steep to raise cattle or grow crops. They can survive in any climate in Britain.

Sheep often live in areas where soils are thin and have little goodness in them. They feed mainly on grass, heather and other poor-quality vegetation. Most hill sheep farms like mine are very large but make little use of modern machinery.

C

Cattle farming

We have two herds of cows. One is for milk and dairy products and the other one for beef. Cows need land that is quite well drained and is either flat or gently sloping. They feed on grass, which grows best in a moist, warm climate.

Dairy farms need to be next to good roads so that the milk can be quickly transported to nearby markets. Refrigerated milk lorries help to keep milk fresh and enable it to be transported longer distances.

D

Mixed farming

Mixed farms need good-quality soil and a climate that is neither too wet nor too dry. These factors help grass and crop growth. Good roads and a nearby market where we can sell our produce, are also important.

We grow crops and raise livestock. Our farm is ideal for mixed farming as most of it is flat or gently sloping. This is good for the cattle and makes it easy to use modern machinery when ploughing the fields or harvesting crops.

Activities

1 Match the following beginnings to the correct endings.

Arable farming	is rearing animals
Pastoral farming	is rearing animals and growing crops
Mixed farming	is growing crops

2 Diagram **E** shows some newspaper headlines about problems which affect farming. Copy table **F** below and sort the headlines in **E** into the correct columns.

F

Problems which affect farming	
Physical	Human

E

Wet summers cause disease in potatoes

Ferry strike – fruit rots in French ports

Sheep are stranded in snowdrifts

Farms are too small for family to earn a living

Crops ruined by flooding

Fruit blossoms killed by frost

Rise in petrol prices

High electricity prices – dairy farmers with milk machines hit hard

Daffodils flattened by strong winds

Summary

The three main types of farming in Britain are arable, pastoral and mixed. The type of farming that is best for an area depends on several physical and human factors.

What is an arable farm like?

Photo **A** and map **B** show Hawthorn Farm, a typical arable farm in East Anglia. The land here is very flat and slopes gently eastwards towards a river. Most of the fields have deep and **fertile** soils. These are easy to work and are well drained, although occasional flooding restricts the use of land near to the river.

East Anglia is one of the driest parts of Britain. Much of the rain falls in the growing season when it is most needed. Summers are generally warm with plenty of sunshine to ripen the crops. The cold winters have hard frosts which help to kill diseases and break up the soil, which assists ploughing.

The main problems for farmers in the area are occasional high winds and summer thunderstorms that can ruin the crops just before harvest time. Farmers cope with unusually dry summers by **irrigating** the land through a system of ditches, pipes and pumping units. Pumps are also used to move water from the fields and into the river when flooding occurs. Flooding is a problem in the area because the land is so flat and low-lying. Many farmers are concerned that floods happen more often now than they did in the past.

A

Key

	Wheat
	Potatoes
	Sugar beet
	Peas
	Set-aside
	Woodland

Hawthorn Farm

B   An arable farm in East Anglia

The sheep on Beckside Farm spend most of their time on the high fells. Life here is hard and only strong, healthy sheep survive. In winter, when conditions on the mountainside are uncertain, weaker sheep are brought down to lower pastures.

The small area of lowland is well used. The fields are ploughed each year and fertiliser added to improve the soil's fertility and structure. Oats, barley and turnips are grown during the summer and stored in the large barns. These are then given to the sheep as winter feed.

Beckside Farm earns most of its money in the autumn when lambs and four-year-old sheep are taken to the nearby market at Penrith. Wool is sold in summer but is no longer a main source of income.

Making a living on a hill sheep farm is difficult, so both the Government and the European Union provide **subsidies** for the farmer. These come mainly in the form of grants and loans. Even with this help, many hill sheep farmers still struggle to survive.

In the harsh, rough grazing of the fells, only hardy breeds of sheep can be reared. The **Herdwick** is the toughest breed of sheep in Britain and can cope well with wet and cold conditions. It has a thick grey fleece and is long-lived. The **Swaledale** is now the most common breed in the Lake District. It is hardy and has good lambing and breeding ability.

C

Activities

1 Look at diagram **D**, showing the farmer's year.
   a) Which are the four warmest months?
   b) Which are the four wettest months?
   c) How much rainfall is there in January?
   d) When do the sheep need extra food? Suggest reasons for this.

2 Make a fact file to show the main features of a hill sheep farm. Use the headings shown here.

Hill sheep farm
- Location ...
- Relief ...
- Soils ...
- Climate ...
- Method ...
- Use of machinery ...
- Source of income ...
- Difficulties ...

Diagram D — The farmer's year: hill sheep farming

DECEMBER — Winter feed started — 3
JANUARY — Winter feed given — 3
NOVEMBER — Dipping and mating — 6
FEBRUARY — Winter feed given — 3
OCTOBER — Surplus ewes and lambs sold — 8
MARCH — Flock gathered. Vaccinations — 5
SEPTEMBER — New lambs taken from sheep — 12
APRIL — Lambing begins — 7
AUGUST — Fleeces sold — 14
— Sheep returned to fell — 9
MAY
JULY — Shearing and dipping — 14
JUNE — 12

Rainfall scale: 50, 100, 150, 200

D The farmer's year: hill sheep farming

Key
▢ Rainfall (mm)
Total rainfall 1,880 mm
⑭ Temperature (°C)

Summary

Harsh conditions and poor land quality make farming difficult in upland areas. Hill sheep farming is common in places where it is not possible to raise cattle or grow crops.

What is the distribution pattern of farming in Britain?

We have seen how the type and methods of farming are influenced by physical and human factors. As these factors can change within a few kilometres, so too can the type of farming. To draw a detailed and accurate map to show where the main farming types are found in Britain would be very complicated. It is often more meaningful to draw a simplified, or generalised, map instead.

Map **A** is generalised. It is easy to draw and to understand. However, if you look at an atlas map showing 'farming in Britain' you will see several important differences which the generalised map cannot show. These include arable farming in eastern Scotland, sheep on the Pennines and market gardening in Lancashire.

A ▸ **Simplified map showing the distribution of farming types in Britain**

Crofting

Towards the north and west

- More wind
- Cooler summers
- Milder winters
- More rain
- Higher land
- Steeper slopes
- Thinner soils
- More extensive farming
- More subsistence farming

Sheep

Crofting

Sheep

Cattle

Mixed

Arable

Cattle

Mixed

Arable

Towards the south and east

- More sheltered
- Warmer summers
- Colder winters
- Less rain
- Flatter land
- More gentle slopes
- Deeper soil
- More intensive farming
- More commercial farming

How is this distribution pattern changing?

The most recent changes have resulted from decisions made by the European Union (the EU) in Brussels. For example, since the mid-1970s there has been a rapid increase in farm cultivation of **oilseed rape** in Britain (photo **B**). This crop is grown for several reasons:

- Britain and the EU are short of oilseed.
- Oilseed is used to make margarine and cooking oil. By producing our own oil, shop prices are kept lower.
- Farmers get a high price for oilseed.
- After harvesting, the remains can be fed to cattle.
- Rape puts goodness (nitrogen) back into the soil and so is an ideal rotation crop.

B

Although some parts of the world are short of food, Britain and the EU have been producing too much. When too much food is produced it is called a **surplus**. This surplus food is not sold to poorer countries but is stored. Stores of food like butter, wheat and beef are called **food mountains**. Reserves of liquids like milk, wine and olive oil are called **food lakes**. To try to get rid of these 'mountains' and 'lakes' the EU has reduced money paid to farmers (**subsidies**). Farmers are now paid money to use their land in other ways. Two of these are shown in diagrams **C** and **D**.

C

Set-aside land

£200 per hectare per year is given to arable farmers if they stop growing crops for five years on over 20% of their land. The land can be left under grass, sold as building land or turned into woodland. Most farmers who have accepted this offer are leaving their land under grass (fallow).

D

Farm woodland scheme

Farmers are given a grant of up to £190 per hectare to plant trees on land which they used to farm. Up to 505 conifers and 1,375 deciduous trees can be planted on each hectare.

Activities

1 Five types of farming are shown on map **A**. Match each type with the following five descriptions.
- Animals kept for milk and meat
- A subsistence form of farming
- Growing crops
- Growing crops and rearing animals
- Hill farming

2 **a)** What is oilseed rape?
   b) Give four reasons why it has become an important crop in Britain.

3 Diagram **E** shows food surpluses as 'mountains' and 'lakes'.
   a) What is a food surplus?
   b) Draw the diagram and then label:
   - three products which make 'mountains'
   - three products which form 'lakes'.

E

'Mountains'

'Lakes'

E X T R A

You are an arable farmer. The EU decides to give you less money for your crops. Would you:
- still go on growing crops
- 'set-aside' some land as grass (fallow) or
- plant several hectares of trees?
Give reasons for your decision.

Summary

It is possible to recognise a generalised distribution pattern of farming in Britain. This pattern has taken centuries to develop and is still changing.

How has farming changed the landscape?

Most of southern Britain was once covered in forest and marshland. As farming developed the forests were cleared and the marshes were drained. Later, hedges were planted and stone walls built. These created the fields which we now think of as being typical of farming areas.

Recently many more changes have taken place in our landscape. Sketch **A** shows some of the changes which have taken place in the last 60 years.

A

1940s

2000s

It is the farmers' job to try to produce more of our food. To do so they have drained **wetlands** and cleared **hedgerows**. These two changes have upset many people.

Wetlands are marshy areas. They also form one of the last of our natural environments, providing homes for a wide variety of

wildlife. As wetlands are drained, mainly for pastoral farming, the habitats of many birds, insects, animals and plants are destroyed.

Hedges were planted to stop animals from wandering and to show boundaries of land. Many people consider hedges to be very important to the environment. While farmers may share these views, it is their land which is taken up by hedges and their job to look after them. Since 1945, about one kilometre of hedge out of every four has been cleared (diagram **B**). Every cleared kilometre gives one extra hectare of land. (Remember some farms in India are only that size!)

B

Hedges in Britain

100%

1945

70%

1995

C Advantages and disadvantages of hedges

Well looked after hedges are attractive

Hedge roots hold the soil together and reduce erosion

Hedges provide a home for wildlife

Cutting hedges costs the farmer time and money. A hedgecutter costs over £7,000

Hedges take up space which could be used for farmland

Hedges get in the way of big machinery in fields

Photo **D** shows soil erosion in central England. This happens when soil is no longer protected by the hedges. In this case it is blown away by very strong winds.

Activities

1 **Spot the differences** in the two sketches in **A**. Try to find one difference for each of the following: *field size, farm buildings, machinery, hedgerows, wetlands.*

2 Find a partner in your class. One of you will be a farmer, the other will be a conservationist.
   a) If you are the farmer, say:
   ● why you planted hedges in the first place
   ● why you now wish to remove them.

   b) If you are the conservationist, explain why you feel it is very important to keep the hedges.
   Both of you should get help from photo **C**.

Find out what is meant by **soil erosion**. Why are parts of eastern England affected by soil erosion when it is very windy? Apart from losing it by wind, how else may farmers lose their soil?

Summary

The present appearance of much of Britain's landscape is the result of farming. As farming changes, then so too does our landscape.

How has farming changed?

Farming, like any industry, has to change with the times. It has to keep up with modern methods, provide the produce that people want, look after the countryside, and ensure a living for its workers.

In the last 40 years or so, changes in farming have been more rapid than in the past. Some of these are shown in cartoon **A** below.

The most visible change in farming is that farms are now much bigger. This makes them more efficient. Fields are also larger so that machinery can be used and huge areas given to one crop. The greater use of fertiliser, pesticides and improved seeds has also helped increase the amount of food produced.

However, modern agricultural methods have brought some serious problems. The introduction of machinery has reduced the number of farm workers needed. The use of chemicals has damaged the environment and **wildlife habitats** and **plant communities** have been destroyed.

Efforts have been made to reduce this damage through the introduction of several government initiatives. These include **set-aside land** and farm **woodland projects** as described on page 35. The Countryside Stewardship scheme is a more recent approach. Through this, farmers are paid to repair walls, replant hedges, create footpaths and restore damaged habitats.

In 2001, foot and mouth disease affected up to 2,000 farms, led to the slaughter of 6 million animals, and cost agriculture £1 billion. Some farmers left the industry while others, encouraged by the government, developed more varied approaches.

Farmers

Prices have fallen so we do not make so much money.

Many farmers faced ruin after foot and mouth disease.

The EU is giving us less money for our produce, especially cereals and milk.

New machinery is too expensive for us to afford it.

The rapid increase in fuel prices has cost us a lot of money.

We now earn only just enough money to cover our yearly running costs.

Townspeople

We want farmers to reduce the amount of fertiliser and pesticides they use.

We do not want farmers to grow crops that have been genetically modified.

We would prefer natural, organic crops but do not want to pay high prices.

We want farmers to restore hedges and wetlands for wildlife.

We want access to the countryside and to be able to walk where we want.

Despite the improvements in farming methods and the increase in yields, many farmers still struggle to make a living and many have even gone out of business. Some of the more inventive have developed leisure activities to bring in money and subsidise their incomes. These developments tend to be more successful in tourist areas and near towns rather than in the more remote locations. Cartoon **B** shows some typical activities on these so-called leisure farms.

B

Activities

C

1 Look at the graphs in **C**.
   a) Describe the changes in farming shown by each of the graphs.
   b) What is the link between the number of tractors and the number of farmworkers? Why do you think there is this link?

2 Write two letters to your local newspaper. Each letter should be about half a page in length.
   a) In the first letter give the views of the farmers who are concerned that producing food and making a living is becoming increasingly difficult.
   b) In the second letter give the views of townspeople who would like farmers to use methods that are less damaging to the environment.

3 **a)** Why are some farmers developing leisure activities on their farms?
   b) Draw a star diagram to show some of the leisure activities available on a farm.

Summary

There have been many changes to farming in recent years. These changes have brought benefits but they have also caused problems.

The farming enquiry

Farmers have to make decisions about what kind of farming they are going to do. They have to choose carefully what crops they will grow or what livestock they may keep. It is important that these decisions are good ones, or the farmer will find it difficult to produce food efficiently and make a living.

In this unit we have seen how the type of farming can be influenced by factors such as climate, relief, soils, transport and government policies. These factors are not the same everywhere but vary from place to place. This helps explains why there are differences in farming types across the country.

In this enquiry, your task is to help four farmers choose the type of farming that is most suited to the farm they have recently purchased. To do this you will need to look closely at the features of each farm and match these to the requirements of the different kinds of farming.

Mr McNeish of Achantee Farm

Mr and Mrs Carr of Brechie Farm

Mr Tregoglas of Cutford Farm

Mr and Mrs Nash of Dalton Farm

There should be three main parts to your enquiry:
- The first part will be an introduction where you will explain what the enquiry is about.
- In the second part you will need to collect and present information to help you make your decisions.
- Finally you will need a conclusion. Here you will choose the type of farming for each location and answer the following enquiry question:

How and why does farming vary in different parts of Britain?

A What type of farming?

Farming type	Climate needs	Relief	Soil	Other
Arable Grain crops and vegetables, mainly for human use. Some used as animal feed.	Most crops grow best with: • 650–800 mm of rainfall • summer temperatures above 15°C for ripening and harvesting • sunshine to ripen crops.	Flat or gently sloping so that machinery may be used easily.	Deep and fertile soils that are easy to work	Near to urban markets and good transport links. Able to use machinery.
Dairying Cattle kept for milk and for making dairy products like cheese and yoghurt.	Good grass needed all year: • more than 800 mm of rain • warm summers • winter temperatures above 6°C for continuous grass growth.	Hilly or gently sloping land. Cows have difficulty on steep ground.	Moisture-retaining for good grass growth.	Near to urban markets and accessible for milk tankers.
Beef cattle Fattened for meat.	Feed mainly on rough pasture. Grass is useful in summer for fattening: • more than 700 mm of rainfall • warm or mild summers.	Hilly or gently sloping land. Cows have difficulty on steep ground.	Can survive on poorer soils if not waterlogged.	Accessible to urban areas for processing. Transport links to markets.
Hill sheep Kept for meat and wool.	Sheep graze on rough pasture. They are hardy animals and can put up with high rainfall (1,500 mm or more), snow, and low winter temperatures.	Sheep are able to graze steep and mountainous land.	Areas of better soil can provide winter feed.	Good access to markets and transport links not so important.

A

Achantee Farm is in north-west Scotland some 45 minutes by road from Fort William. The roads here are narrow and travel can be difficult. Farmland is mountainous with steep slopes and poor soils. The farm has a small area of flat land on the valley floor close to the river. The soil is deeper here but can be waterlogged in winter.

Brechie Farm is in north-east Scotland on the edge of the Cairngorm Mountains. The land on the farm is hilly but the soils are deep and fertile. There is some good-quality grass on the valley floor, but most of the land is rough pasture. The roads are quite good and Aberdeen, the nearest large town, has rail links to Edinburgh and the south.

Cutford Farm is in Devon in south-west England. The farm has quite small fields surrounded by high hedgerows with narrow country lanes between them. The countryside is very hilly but the soil is rich and well drained. The M4 motorway is just 5 km away and Exeter, the nearest large town, less than 30 minutes' drive from the farm.

Dalton Farm is close to Cambridge in south-east England. The land here is mostly flat with some gently sloping hills. The farm covers a huge area and has large fields with deep, fertile soil. The M11 motorway runs alongside the farm and there are good rail connections between Cambridge, London and other parts of the country.

1 Introduction – what is the enquiry about?

You will need to use maps and writing here. Star diagrams or lists might also help.

a) First look carefully at the enquiry question and say what you are going to find out.
- Describe the main types of farming and their different requirements.
- Explain how the factors that affect farming vary across the country so that some areas are more suited to certain types of farming than others.

b) Describe briefly the main features of the four different farms. Show on a map where they are located.

C Climate conditions

Achantee Farm
Mild summers (14°C)
Mild winters (6°C)
Very wet (1,980 mm) and mostly cloudy all year round

Brechie Farm
Mild summers (15°C)
Cold winters (4°C)
Quite dry (750 mm)
Some winter snow

Cutford Farm
Warm summers (16°C)
Mild winters (7°C)
Quite wet (960 mm)
Fine summers, cloudy winters

Dalton Farm
Warm summers (17°C)
Cold winters (5°C)
Dry (650 mm)
Plenty of summer sunshine

2 What type of farming is most suitable?

a) Decide the type of farming most suited to each farm based only on climatic needs. Table **A** and map **C** will help you.

b) Now consider other farming needs and check that your choice of farms is still suitable. Table **A** and diagram **B** will help you.

c) Make a copy of the farm fact file **D** and complete it to explain your choice of farming. Complete similar fact files for the other farms.

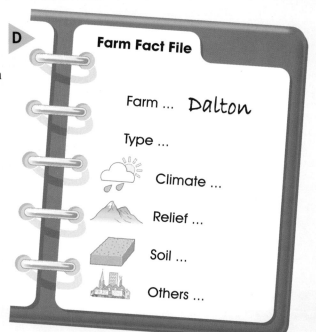

D

Farm Fact File

Farm ... *Dalton*

Type ...

Climate ...

Relief ...

Soil ...

Others ...

3 Conclusion

Now you should look carefully at your work and answer the enquiry question. There could be two parts to this section.

a) First, you could write a short letter to each farmer suggesting what type of farming would be most suited to his farm, and giving reasons for your choice.

b) Second, you could describe and suggest reasons for the differences in farming in Britain. This could include writing and a labelled map.

E

3 Secondary activities

What are secondary activities?

We have already seen that primary industry makes up one group of economic activities (page 24). **Primary industries** are those economic activities that collect or produce natural resources obtained from the land or sea. A second group of economic activities are **secondary industries**. This is when people make things from natural resources. Another name for these industries is **manufacturing**. Manufacturing usually takes place in **factories**. Secondary industry also includes putting together (**assembling** and **constructing**) manufactured goods. Four examples of secondary activities are shown in **A**, **B**, **C** and **D**.

A third group of economic activities are the **tertiary industries**. These provide a service, such as selling the manufactured goods.

A

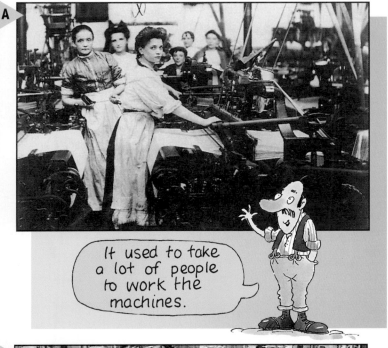

It used to take a lot of people to work the machines.

B

A modern factory where people need a lot of skill.

C

A modern car assembly plant where very few people are needed to work the machines.

D

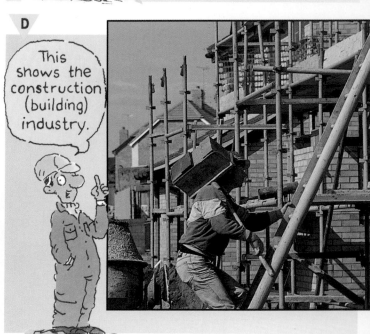

This shows the construction (building) industry.

In the UK most people now work in either secondary or tertiary occupations. As the graphs in **E** show, however, this has not always been the case.

Before 1800 most people earned a living from the land. The majority were farmers although a few made products that the farmer needed, such as farm equipment, or produced foodstuffs like flour and bread.

During the nineteenth century people turned to industry. An increasing number worked in factories making things like steel, ships and machinery. This was the time of the industrial revolution.

Further changes occurred during the twentieth century and up to the present day. Farming and industry have become more mechanised and need fewer workers. Many people now work in service activities such as in schools, hospitals and shops. Transport has also provided many jobs.

The proportion of people working in primary, secondary and tertiary activities is called the **employment structure**.

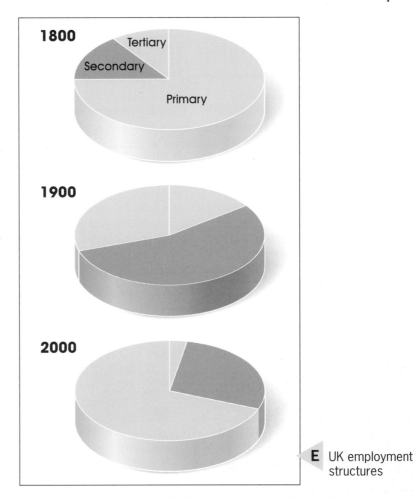

E UK employment structures

Activities

1 Match the following beginnings with the correct endings.

Beginnings	Endings
Primary activities	make things from natural resources
Secondary activities	collect natural resources from the sea or land
Tertiary activities	are grown, found in the sea or dug from the ground
Natural resources	provide a service for people

2 Look at the list of jobs in box **F**. Sort them into primary, secondary and tertiary activities.

3 a) Complete a survey of people in your class to find out one job that a member of each person's family does.
 b) Sort the jobs into primary, secondary and tertiary.
 c) Draw a bar graph to show your findings.
 d) Describe what your bar graph shows.

F

TV presenter, coal miner, nurse, shoemaker, footballer, forestry worker, fire fighter, bus driver, carpenter, fisherman, police officer, baker, shop assistant, oilrig worker, quarry worker, farmer, pop singer, builder, sewing machinist

Summary   Secondary activities employ people to make or manufacture things from natural resources. Most secondary activity takes place in factories.

45

What is the best site for a factory?

Before building a factory a manufacturer should try to work out the best site for its location. It is unusual to find a perfect site for a factory. Indeed, if there was a perfect site someone else would probably already be using it. Deciding on the best available site depends on several things. Six of these are given in sketch **A**.

A

1 My factory uses lots of **raw materials**. It costs money and takes time to move them so it is best if my factory is as close as possible to these materials. This is even more important if the materials are big and heavy.

2 My factory needs lots of **power** (energy) to work the machines. When the factory was first built a fast flowing river powered the machines. Now we use electricity.

3 A few years ago many people (**labour**) were needed to work in my factory. Today a few machines can do most of this work. However, my present small labour force must be trained and skilled.

4 The best place for any factory is near to a large urban **market**. A market is where most of the people who buy the goods live.

5 **Transport** was a very important factor in choosing the site for my factory. It is needed to bring raw materials and workers to the factory and to send manufactured goods to the market.

6 The **site** for the factory is good because there is plenty of cheap flat land there.

Textiles are often the first industry to be developed in a country. In Britain the first two important textile areas were in East Anglia and the Cotswolds. Later the industry moved to Yorkshire and Lancashire because these areas had more advantages. Yorkshire became important for woollen textiles and Lancashire for cotton textiles. Sketch **B** shows why parts of Yorkshire gave the best location for woollen mills (factories).

B
The best location for a textile mill

2 The Pennines get a lot of rain. Rivers flowing from these hills were fast flowing and could power machinery. Later coal was found here and this replaced water power.

1 Raw materials were easy to get. The mills used wool from sheep reared on the Pennines. Water for washing the wool came from local rivers.

3 At this time Britain's population was growing rapidly (pages 84–99). Many people needed work and so moved to find jobs in the textile mills.

6 Flat land next to the river made this a good site.

5 Canals were built next to rivers. Canals were used to move both raw materials and manufactured goods. Later railways and roads were built.

4 As Britain's population increased so did the need for clothes. Textiles were needed by people in the growing urban markets both at home and overseas.

Activities

1 Match these beginnings to the correct endings.

Raw materials are	needed to move raw materials, people and goods.
Power is	a place where manufactured goods are sold.
Labour is	needed to work machines.
A market is	natural resources from which goods are made.
Transport is	people who work in factories.

2 Choose **either** a factory near to where you live **or** the woollen textile mill described on this page. Using diagram **C** as a guide, explain why the factory or mill grew at that site.

C

Name the raw materials. Where do they come from?

Describe the type of transport used

Name the type of power

Mill or factory

Where are the markets?

Describe the land at the site

Where do the workers come from? Are many needed?

Summary

In choosing the best site to locate a factory, a manufacturer should consider transport and the nearness to raw materials, power sources, workers, and markets for its goods.

Choosing the right site — the iron and steel industry

Industries near to raw materials

Britain was the first country in the world to become **industrialised**. Industrialisation began about 200 years ago after the discovery that coal could be used to produce steam and that steam could be used to work machines. Machines did many of the jobs previously done by people.

In those days transport was poor. There were no lorries or trains, no motorways or railways. Coal and other raw materials were heavy and expensive to move. This meant that most early industries grew up on Britain's coalfields (map **A**). The most important industry became the production of iron and, after 1856, steel.

The iron and steel industry

Three raw materials are needed to make iron and steel – iron ore, coal and, in smaller amounts, limestone. Coke, from coal, is used to **smelt** (melt) the iron ore. This is done because iron ore contains impurities such as carbon. Limestone is added to help separate the pure

iron from the impurities, leaving steel behind. Diagram **B** shows what was needed to make one tonne of steel in the nineteenth century.

This meant that early ironworks were located on coalfields where iron ore was found nearby (map **A**).

When steel was made instead of iron, steelworks still favoured coalfield locations. Steel was used to make things like ships, trains, bridges and textile machinery. As these industries grew in size and number, many people moved to them to find work. Most coalfields became crowded with people. Today many of these early industrial areas have used up their raw materials. Their industries are in decline, factories have closed, it is hard for people to find jobs, and the environment has often been left spoilt.

A **Location of iron and coalfields**

Key
▓ Coalfields
■ Iron ore
S Early iron and steel areas

0   100   200 km

Scottish
S

North-east
S   S
S
Yorkshire, Derby
and Nottingham
Western
S
South Staffs
and Midlands
South
Wales
S
Kent

B

8 tonnes of coal   +   4 tonnes of iron ore   +   1 tonne of limestone   =   1 tonne of steel

C Pouring molten steel

D Newly made sheet steel

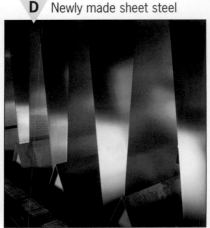

Britain's largest steelworks is at Port Talbot on the coast of South Wales near to Swansea. Steel has been made here since 1901 when the first steelworks was built. Port Talbot's main product is sheet steel which is used in the car industry, and for making household goods such as washing machines.

So what makes Port Talbot such a good site for a steelworks? Photo **E** shows some of the major reasons. A further important reason is that the government was keen to provide work in an area where many people at the time were out of work and needed jobs.

E Port Talbot – an ideal site for a steelworks?

Port facilities for import of raw materials and export of steel to foreign markets

Ample supply of water for cooling

Good rail links to UK car factories

Large flat site available on coastal plain

Many skilled workers living in local area

Electric power available through the National Grid

Coking coal and limestone available locally

M4 motorway access to UK markets

Activities

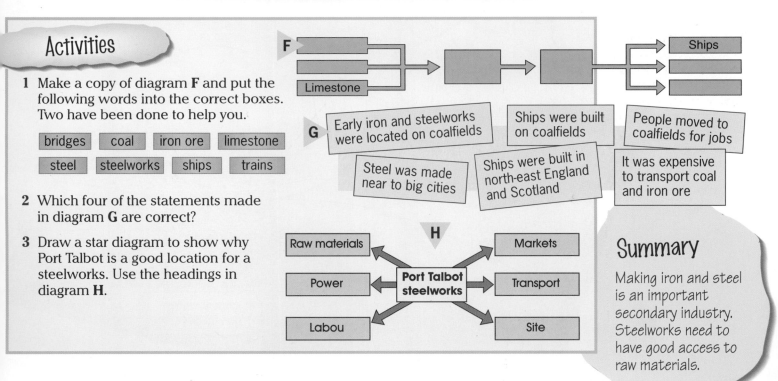

1 Make a copy of diagram **F** and put the following words into the correct boxes. Two have been done to help you.

| bridges | coal | iron ore | limestone |

| steel | steelworks | ships | trains |

2 Which four of the statements made in diagram **G** are correct?

3 Draw a star diagram to show why Port Talbot is a good location for a steelworks. Use the headings in diagram **H**.

F

Limestone · Ships

G
Early iron and steelworks were located on coalfields

Ships were built on coalfields

People moved to coalfields for jobs

Steel was made near to big cities

Ships were built in north-east England and Scotland

It was expensive to transport coal and iron ore

H
Raw materials · Markets
Power · **Port Talbot steelworks** · Transport
Labou · Site

Summary

Making iron and steel is an important secondary industry. Steelworks need to have good access to raw materials.

How can the ideal site for an industry change?

A factory should try to make a profit. We have already seen (page 46) that before building a factory a manufacturer should work out the best site to locate it. However, the advantages available when locating a textile mill or an iron works in the early 1800s may no longer exist today. This means that the ideal site for a new textile factory or a modern steelworks will have changed.

Changes in the iron and steel industry

Diagram **A** shows a part of Britain which has always been important for making iron and, after 1856, steel. It also shows that while the best sites for the early iron industry were inland, the best location for a modern steelworks is near to the coast.

A

Railway opened 1850

Y

Coal-mine opened 1810, closed 1890

Attractive hilly area with several limestone quarries

W

Iron ore mined 1820–1920

Canal opened 1820

River

X

Z

Large town with port facilities

S

Sea

Activities

1 **In 1820** an iron manufacturer decided to build an ironworks in the area shown on diagram **A**. The manufacturer had to choose between sites **W**, **X**, **Y** and **Z**.

Some of the factors that had to be considered when choosing the site are listed in matrix **C**. The manufacturer eventually chose site **W** for the ironworks. To see why that site was chosen, try completing the matrix yourself.

a) Look carefully at diagram **A** and box **B**. For the first location factor give a score for each site. Do the same for each of the other location factors. Part of the matrix has been done to help you.

b) Add up the scores. The one with the highest total will be the best site. It should be site **W**. Give four reasons why **W** was a good site for an ironworks in 1820.

2 **By 1990** the factory at **W** no longer made a profit. It was too small and the coal and iron ore in the area had run out. These raw materials were now brought in from abroad by sea. It was decided that the factory had to be enlarged or a new steelworks built either at site **Z** or **S**.

Matrix **D** shows some of the factors that the manufacturer had to consider before deciding whether to stay at **W** or go to **Z** or **S**. You decide what should be done by completing the matrix. Remember that it is much cheaper to expand at the same place than to build a new factory at a different site.

a) Complete the matrix using the scoring from box **B**.

b) Did you decide to expand at **W** or did you choose one of the sites **Z** or **S**?

c) Write a short paragraph giving the reasons for your decision.

B

Give a score of 0 to 4 for each site.

4 if the site is **excellent**

3 if the site is **very good**

2 if the site is **good** but has faults

1 if the site is **poor** and only just acceptable

0 if the site is **unsatisfactory**

C

Location factors for ironworks in 1820	Site W	Site X	Site Y	Site Z
Near to local iron ore	4			1
Near to local coal		2		
Near to local limestone				
River or canal needed for transport	4			
Flat land needed for factory				4
Close to town for workers				
Total				

D

Location factors for steelworks in 1990	Site W	Site Z	Site S
Near to port for coal and iron imports			
Near to local limestone			
Railways and roads needed for transport			
Flat, cheap land needed for factory			
Near town for skilled workers			
Same or different location			
Total			

Summary   The best site for an industry changes as location factors change. The British iron industry grew up near raw materials. Britain's few remaining steelworks are located near to the coast.

Choosing the right site — the car industry

Industries near to markets

As raw materials are used up, and as transport improves, then modern factories tend to locate in areas where many people live. This is mainly because present-day industries need large markets in which to sell their goods. The car industry is an example of an industry that is building new factories near to markets.

The car industry

A modern car consists of many small parts. Each part is made in its own factory. If the factories making these parts are all close together then it is easier and cheaper for the car manufacturer to **assemble** (put together) all of these parts. If large towns are nearby then workers from these towns can make and assemble the parts and, hopefully, buy many of the finished cars. Transport is important for moving car parts, assembled cars and workers. Map **A** shows where most people in Britain live and where the largest car assembly plants are located.

Today industrial growth is more likely in those areas where there are most people. In these places new factories are opening, jobs are easier to get, and more care is taken of the environment.

A Location of car assembly plants

Key

■ Areas with most people

Car assembly plants
- ● Austin Rover
- ● Vauxhall
- ○ Ford
- ● Peugeot-Talbot
- ● Japanese links

0   100   200 km

Washington (Nissan)

Liverpool   Leyland

Ellesmere Port   Derby (Toyota)

Birmingham   Coventry

Oxford   Luton

Bridgend   Swindon (Honda)   Dagenham

Southampton

B A car assembly line

Toyota is Japan's largest car company. In the early 1990s it decided to build a new car manufacturing plant at Burnaston near Derby. The plant opened in 1992 and in 2001 was producing 200,000 cars a year with a workforce of 3,300 people. Most Toyota cars are sold in the UK and Europe. Some are even transported to Japan to be sold there.

Toyota use a **just-in-time** system of manufacture where components (car parts) are supplied to the assembly line just minutes before they are needed. Expensive parts do not have to be stored on site so costs are reduced. Just-in-time needs a good transport system for it to work. Map **C** shows some reasons why Toyota chose Burnaston.

C Burnaston – an ideal site for a car manufacturer?

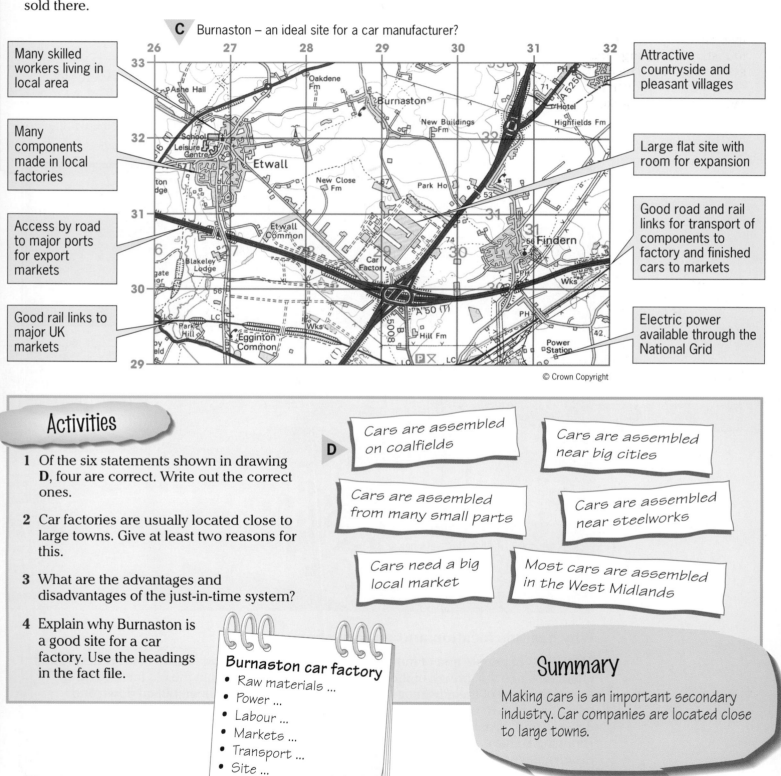

Many skilled workers living in local area

Many components made in local factories

Access by road to major ports for export markets

Good rail links to major UK markets

Attractive countryside and pleasant villages

Large flat site with room for expansion

Good road and rail links for transport of components to factory and finished cars to markets

Electric power available through the National Grid

© Crown Copyright

Activities

1 Of the six statements shown in drawing **D**, four are correct. Write out the correct ones.

2 Car factories are usually located close to large towns. Give at least two reasons for this.

3 What are the advantages and disadvantages of the just-in-time system?

4 Explain why Burnaston is a good site for a car factory. Use the headings in the fact file.

D

Cars are assembled on coalfields

Cars are assembled near big cities

Cars are assembled from many small parts

Cars are assembled near steelworks

Cars need a big local market

Most cars are assembled in the West Midlands

Burnaston car factory
- Raw materials …
- Power …
- Labour …
- Markets …
- Transport …
- Site …

Summary

Making cars is an important secondary industry. Car companies are located close to large towns.

Industries in the inner city

Before industrialisation began in Britain, many towns in Wales, Scotland and the north of England were small. As industry grew so did the need for workers. When the workers moved to the towns to find jobs they needed houses in which to live. At that time there were no private cars or buses so people had to walk to work. It was best for them if they lived near to the factory or mill in which they worked (photo **A**). So in the early nineteenth century both industry and terraced housing grew up on what were then the edges of towns. Since then towns have continued to grow. Those early industries and houses have been surrounded by newer buildings, leaving them in what we now call the 'inner city'.

Until recently most industries were still located in the inner cities. Indeed, as drawing **B** shows, there were still several good points to those industries having a location there.

A

B

Early good points

Cheap houses for poorly paid workers and immigrants

Near to CBD

Nearby terraced houses for workers

Canal carried heavy goods

Many workers needed many houses

Railways helped movement of heavy goods

Waste deposited into river

River water used for cooling

Why has this location and pattern changed?

The needs of people and of industry have changed since the growth of those early factories. Many of the advantages of having a location near to the city centre have now disappeared. What were once advantages (drawing **B**) have now often become disadvantages (drawing **C**).

Many inner cities have been **redeveloped**. This means that the old factories and houses have been pulled down and replaced either by new buildings or by a different type of land use (drawing **D**). Modern industry now finds that it has more advantages in locating on the edges of towns and cities.

Later bad points ◄ C

Lack of workers as people move out of the area

Houses old, run down, and some vandalised

Old narrow roads often congested

Waste land, dirty environment

Canal not used full of rubbish

Factory is old – has no room to expand

D ►

Small new industries

Some houses cleared for open space

What may be done

DIY superstore

Government grant for redeveloping inner city

New dual carriageway

Canal cleared for leisure barges

Old railways and wasteland cleared and landscaped

Factory is now an industrial museum

Activities

1 Eight points are made in diagram **E** about the location of a factory in an inner city area.

a) List four points which were important when the factory was first built.

b) List four points which show present-day problems for a factory located in an inner city area.

Drawings **B** and **C** will help you with your answer.

E ►

1820

NOW OPEN
Apply within

Workers could afford the small, cheap houses

Near to houses where workers lived

Narrow roads often congested

Canal and river polluted with rubbish and waste

Near to city centre

Next to canal and railway for moving raw materials

No room for factory to expand

1990

FOR SALE

Houses are old, some have been vandalised

2 Compare drawings **B** and **D**. List four ways in which land use in an inner city may have been changed over a period of time.

Summary

There were many advantages for early industry to locate in present-day inner city areas. As many of these advantages no longer exist, the land use of inner cities is changing.

What are high-tech industries?

High-technology or **high-tech industries** make products such as microchips, computers, mobile phones, pharmaceuticals (drugs) and scientific equipment. They have been the growth industry of recent years and now provide more than 25 per cent of the UK's manufacturing jobs.

High-tech companies use the most advanced manufacturing methods. They put great emphasis on the research and development of new products and employ a highly skilled and inventive workforce. Most are huge organisations with offices and factories throughout the world. The UK electronics industry, for example, is controlled almost entirely by foreign companies, mainly from Japan and the USA.

Firms that make high-tech products often group together on pleasant, newly developed **science** or **business parks**. All firms on a science park are high-tech and have direct links with a university. Business parks do not have links with universities and may include superstores, hotels and leisure centres. There are many more business parks than there are science parks.

A Some high-tech companies

Both are located on edge-of-city **greenfield sites** although some business parks are found in inner city areas that have been redeveloped, such as London Docklands. Diagram **B** shows a building on the Cambridge Science Park.

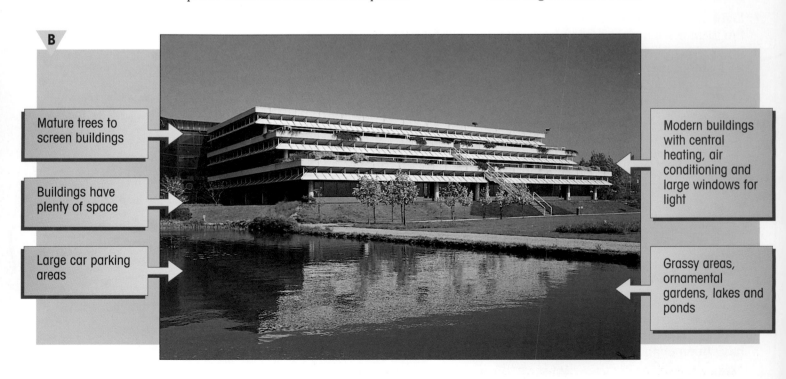

B

Mature trees to screen buildings

Buildings have plenty of space

Large car parking areas

Modern buildings with central heating, air conditioning and large windows for light

Grassy areas, ornamental gardens, lakes and ponds

C

Motorway interchange

Motorway

Hotel

University

Woods

Skilled high-tech workers live nearby on expensive estate

Leisure centre

Grassy areas

Private golf course

City boundary

Cheaper land on edge of city

To city centre

High-tech firms with plenty of room for expansion

Clean, healthy, pleasant environment

Key

Science park

High-tech firm

University campus

Private housing

Trees, woods

Lake, pond

Diagram **C** shows some of the advantages to industry of science and business parks. Others include:

- They should be near to a main road on the edge of town for easy access.
- Nearby firms can exchange ideas and information.
- Leisure facilities and support services may be shared.
- A pool of highly skilled workers can be built up.

There can, however, be some disadvantages. For example:

- An over-use of cars can cause traffic congestion at busy times.
- Edge-of-town sites can be far from shops and services in the town centre.
- Firms may prefer to be by themselves so as to keep new ideas a secret.
- At times it may be difficult for firms to find enough skilled workers.

Activities

1 **a)** What are high-tech industries?
   b) Name five high-tech products that you have used in the last week.

2 Complete table **D** to show the differences between a science park and a business park. Choose your answers from the following pairs:
   a) many/very few
   b) university links/no university links
   c) high-tech firms/high-tech firms, shops, hotels and leisure centres.

3 Using photo **B** and diagram **C**, give six reasons why a high-tech firm should locate on a science park. In your answer you should mention each of the following:
   transport, price of land, the environment, people's health, leisure facilities, exchanging ideas with people from other firms

4 Give two disadvantages which may arise from firms locating in the same place.

Summary

High-tech industries use advanced scientific techniques. They often locate on edge-of-town science or business parks.

D

	Science park	Business park
a		
b		
c		

Where are high-tech industries located?

Industries like shipbuilding, steelmaking, chemical manufacture and textiles used to be very important in the UK. They employed hundreds of thousands of people, mainly in the north and west of the country. These industries are now in decline and large numbers of jobs have been lost as companies have closed down or reduced their output. Industries in decline are often called **sunset industries**.

Sunrise industries are growth industries. They include high-tech industries which use modern factories and often have their own research and development units. High-tech industries have a much freer choice of location than the old traditional industries where nearness to market and raw materials were so important.

The list in **A** shows some of the factors that have to be considered when choosing the location for these industries. A typical site for a high-tech factory is shown in photo **B** which is on a greenfield site, on the edge of a country town, near to a motorway junction and close to a university.

A

High-tech industries like to be located:
- near to motorways or good roads
- near to highly qualified and skilled workers
- near to research facilities in universities
- near to pleasant housing and open space
- near to attractive countryside and good leisure facilities
- near to an airport for international links.

B

Although high-tech companies have factories and research centres in many parts of Britain, three main areas have become particularly important. These are:

1 The M4 corridor following the motorway westwards from London
2 'Silicon Glen' in central Scotland
3 'Silicon Fen' in and around Cambridge.

These locations are shown on maps **C** and **D**.

C

Key
Location of high-tech industry

CENTRAL SCOTLAND (Silicon Glen)

Glasgow
Edinburgh

0   km   200

CAMBRIDGE (Silicon Fen)

M4 CORRIDOR (Silicon Strip)

N

Cardiff
Cambridge
Bristol   London

Key
Area with many high-tech industries
Attractive upland area
☐ University town
✈ Airport
— Motorway

D

A1
M1
M40
Cambridge
Luton ✈   M11
Cotswolds   Chilterns   Stansted ✈
Oxford ☐
Swindon   M25
Brecon Beacons
Heathrow ✈
Newport   M4
Cardiff ✈   Bristol ☐   Reading   London
Severn Estuary   M3   North Downs   M20
Mendips   M23
Gatwick ✈
Exmoor   South Downs   The Channel Tunnel
N
Dartmoor

0   km   100

FRANCE

Activities

1 What are the differences between sunset and sunrise industries?

2 Drawing **E** is a sketch of photo **B**.
   a) Make a larger copy of the sketch.
   b) Colour lightly in pencil: the housing area red, the industrial area brown, the main roads yellow and the countryside green.
   c) Label the features that make the area a good site for a high-tech factory. Write about 10–20 words of explanation for each one.

3 Use the information on map **C** to explain why the M4 corridor is a good location for high-tech industries.

E

Summary High-tech industries can locate in a wide variety of places. Most are found in central Scotland and the south and east of England.

How can industry pollute the environment?

Industry has helped to make Britain one of the richer countries in the world. It makes goods that have improved our standard of living. But industry uses up **resources**, creates waste and can damage the environment.

In the past the main aim of industry was to make a profit. There was little concern or interest in the environment, especially as any damage caused by factories often affected only the local area. People in the main industrial towns of Britain just accepted smoke-filled skies, smoke-stained buildings, dirty rivers with no fish, and piles of coal and other industrial waste, as a normal part of their environment.

Today the effects of industry are so widespread that they are threatening the whole global environment.

Types of industrial pollution

Air

Smoke from chimneys can affect human health by causing breathing problems. Carbon dioxide in smoke is causing world temperatures to rise (see page 79). Other gases in smoke cause acid rain which kills trees and fish.

Water

Factories can allow waste materials to escape into rivers. Industries use water for cooling and return warm water to rivers. This can kill fish.

Visual

Few factories are attractive to look at. When factories close, the land may be left empty (derelict).

Some industries dump their waste materials. Sometimes this waste is dangerous, poisonous or radioactive.

Noise

Lorries going to and from factories, and heavy machinery, create noise for people living nearby.

Smell

Some industries, such as the plastics industry, give off very unpleasant smells.

What can be done to reduce industrial pollution?

One way is by education. As more people become aware of the dangers of pollution, more pressure can be put on industry and governments to prevent further pollution. Results in the last few years have been more encouraging but it is impossible to solve all the problems at once. Likewise, it is impossible to clean up a polluted environment overnight.

A second way is to spend more money on preventing pollution. Unfortunately, not all industries and governments have the money, or the desire, to spend what little money they have on stopping pollution. Factories, and power stations producing energy for industry, can reduce the amount of smoke and gases they give out (page 79). However, this may mean a drop in profits or an increase in the price of goods.

Certainly there is an urgent need to plan and manage our environment more carefully. Prevention is easier than cure.

Activities

1 Look at cartoon **B**.

B

a) Name the five types of pollution shown on the cartoon.
b) What two types of pollution would be the most damaging to plants and wildlife? Give reasons for your answer.
c) Imagine that you lived or worked in this area. Which two types of pollution would you dislike the most? Give reasons.

2 a) How can education help to reduce pollution?
b) Why do many industries not want to spend money on trying to reduce pollution?

3 When applied to pollution, what is meant by the term, 'prevention is easier than the cure'?

E X T R A

Work with a partner and produce a poster to show how industry pollutes the environment. Add a slogan to draw people's attention to these dangers.

Summary

Industry contributes towards air, water, noise, visual and smell pollution. Much education and money are needed to prevent pollution in the future. Cleaning up environments is costly, difficult, and may take a long time.

Industrial location enquiry

This enquiry is concerned with locating a factory. You will find pages 46 to 53 of this book helpful as you work through the enquiry.

In December 1994 the first Toyota car to be made in Europe was driven out of the new factory at Burnaston near Derby. This event followed years of planning and preparation by the Toyota company.

One of the most important decisions that had to be made in the planning process was where to locate the factory. Toyota gave the responsibility of choosing the best site to a small team of experts.

The team began by making a list of location factors for the new factory. They then drew up a shortlist of sites that met the basic requirements. Next they investigated the advantages and disadvantages of each site before finally choosing what they considered to be the best site.

Some of the location factors that the team considered are shown in the drawing below. On the next page are ten possible sites along with information about each one.

Your task in this enquiry is to suggest:
- why Toyota chose the Burnaston site
- how they came to make that choice
- whether their choice was the best one.

Did Toyota choose the best site for their new factory?

We require a very large **site**. To start with we must have at least 2 sq km. We will need more later for expansion. The land needs to be flat and well drained.

Good **communications** are very important to us. We need to be close to a motorway and quite near to a port or airport.

We need a good **workforce**. For this there must be a large number of workers living nearby. There should be good relations between the workforce and the company.

We would like to be located in a pleasant **environment** where our workers can enjoy good living conditions and be near to attractive countryside.

We must have **government aid**. This will help us finance the project, give us support in setting up the factory and provide training for our new workforce.

Possible sites for the Toyota factory

⑤ Warrington
Two large sites (over 3 km²) with planning permission. Skilled workers available. Good labour relations.

④ Speke
Good quality 4 km² site at Liverpool airport. Large workforce available.

③ Shotton
Near Chester. Choice of large sites (over 3km²) but need to be levelled. 16% unemployment. Fair labour relations. Close to Snowdonia National Park.

② Cardiff
1.5 km² flat site. Skilled workers available in nearby large town. Close to National Park.

⑥ Teesside
4 km² site near port used by Nissan. Planning permission for site may be difficult. Large workforce available.

⑦ Humberside
Close to Hull. 1.5 km² site. Needs drainage. Good labour relations but small workforce in area.

⑧ Grimsby
Large flat site near port available. Good labour relations but limited workforce in area.

⑨ Burnaston
Near Derby. Large flat site for use. Skilled workforce available. Good labour relations. Close to Peak District National Park.

① Newport
4 km² flat site next to Llanwern steelworks. 13% unemployment. Near Brecon Beacons National Park.

⑩ East Midlands
Near Northampton. 1 km² flat site. Good labour relations. Can be difficult to find sufficient workers. Near pleasant countryside.

Key
- ◯ Possible site
- ⚓ Main port
- ✈ Airport
- ─── Motorway

0   50   100 km

Main towns and Assisted Areas

The government gives help to industry in Assisted Areas. This may include loans, grants, help with training and provision of services.

Key
- ◯─○ Possible site
- ● Main town
- ▦ Assisted Area

0   100 km

1 Introduction – what is the enquiry about?

You could use diagrams, maps, writing or lists here.

a) Describe what you have to find out in the enquiry.
b) Give a brief background to the new Toyota factory and describe where it is.
c) Explain how the best site may be chosen.

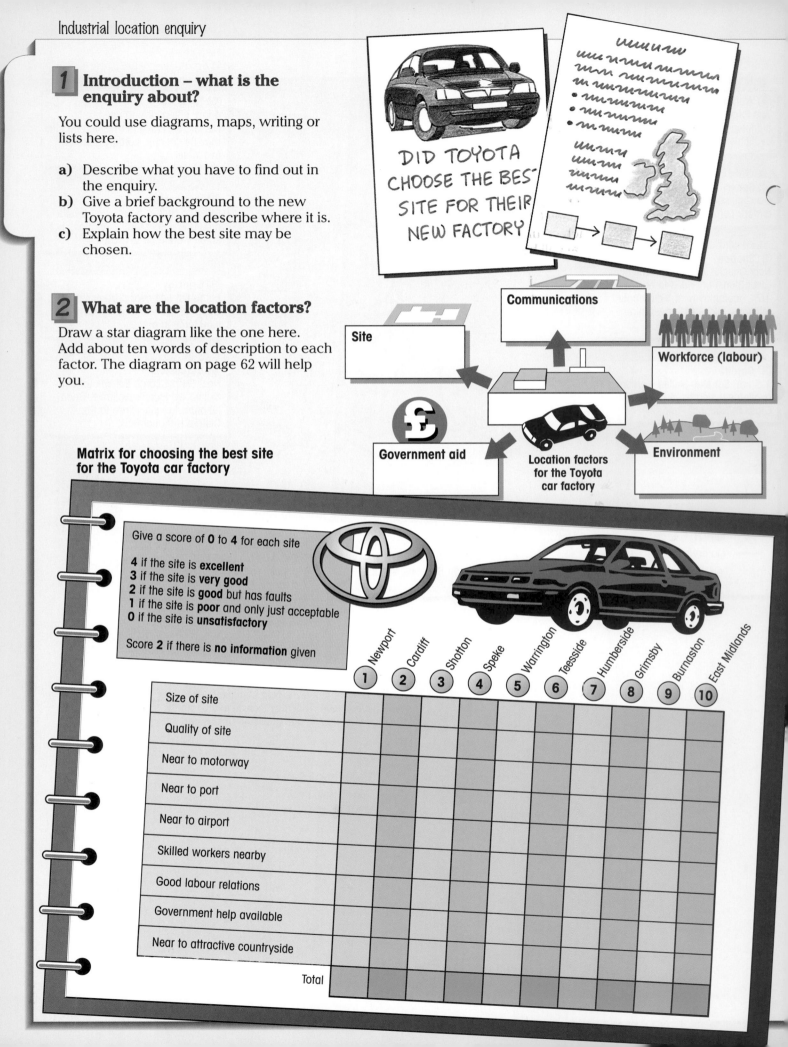

DID TOYOTA CHOOSE THE BEST SITE FOR THEIR NEW FACTORY

2 What are the location factors?

Draw a star diagram like the one here. Add about ten words of description to each factor. The diagram on page 62 will help you.

Site

Communications

Workforce (labour)

Government aid

Environment

Location factors for the Toyota car factory

Matrix for choosing the best site for the Toyota car factory

Give a score of 0 to 4 for each site

4 if the site is **excellent**
3 if the site is **very good**
2 if the site is **good** but has faults
1 if the site is **poor** and only just acceptable
0 if the site is **unsatisfactory**

Score 2 if there is **no information** given

	Newport 1	Cardiff 2	Shotton 3	Speke 4	Warrington 5	Teesside 6	Humberside 7	Grimsby 8	Burnaston 9	East Midlands 10
Size of site										
Quality of site										
Near to motorway										
Near to port										
Near to airport										
Skilled workers nearby										
Good labour relations										
Government help available										
Near to attractive countryside										
Total										

3 Which is the best site?

a) Make a larger copy of the matrix opposite.

b) Look carefully at the information on page 63. For the first location factor give a score for each site. Do the same for each of the other location factors. (The location factors are described more fully on the diagram on page 62.)

c) Add up the scores in each column. The one with the highest total will be the best site.

d) List the ten sites in order of their total scores. Put the best at the top of the list.

4 Conclusion

a) Which are the three best sites? List the main advantages of each one.

b) Suggest why Toyota chose the Burnaston site rather than the other two.

c) If the Burnaston site had not been available, would the other sites have been satisfactory? Give reasons for your answer.

d) **Either**
● Draw a simple sketch of the photo below. Add information to the boxes to explain why Burnaston is a good site for the Toyota car factory. Page 63 and your completed matrix will help you with this.

Or
● Write a report for Head Office in Japan about the Burnaston site. In the report describe the main features of the site and explain why it is a good location for the Toyota car factory.

The Toyota factory at Burnaston near Derby

Workforce (labour)

Site

Government aid

Communications

Environment

Why are we concerned about the environment?

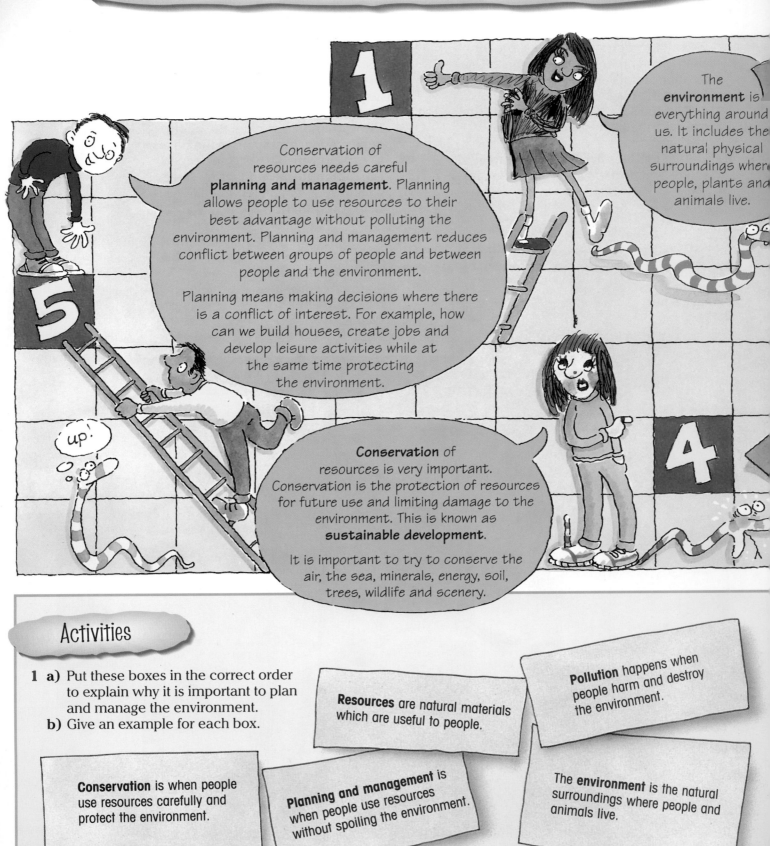

The **environment** is everything around us. It includes the natural physical surroundings where people, plants and animals live.

Conservation of resources needs careful **planning and management**. Planning allows people to use resources to their best advantage without polluting the environment. Planning and management reduces conflict between groups of people and between people and the environment.

Planning means making decisions where there is a conflict of interest. For example, how can we build houses, create jobs and develop leisure activities while at the same time protecting the environment.

Conservation of resources is very important. Conservation is the protection of resources for future use and limiting damage to the environment. This is known as **sustainable development**.

It is important to try to conserve the air, the sea, minerals, energy, soil, trees, wildlife and scenery.

up!

Activities

1 a) Put these boxes in the correct order to explain why it is important to plan and manage the environment.
  b) Give an example for each box.

Resources are natural materials which are useful to people.

Pollution happens when people harm and destroy the environment.

Conservation is when people use resources carefully and protect the environment.

Planning and management is when people use resources without spoiling the environment.

The **environment** is the natural surroundings where people and animals live.

The environment contains **resources** which are materials that occur naturally. They are useful because they can improve people's lives.

Coal, iron ore, clean water, soil, trees, mountains, wildlife and sandy beaches are all examples of resources.

down.!

People must use resources carefully. A careless use may mean that some resources will be **used up**, some will be **wasted**, and some may cause **pollution**. Pollution is when people harm or destroy the natural environment. Pollution can kill plants and animals.

People often misuse these resources. Some resources, like coal, are used up. Some, like forests and soil, are destroyed. Others, like rivers and the air, become polluted.

E X T R A

By yourself, as a group, or as a class, think of one way in which you can try to conserve and protect the environment. Try it out for one week. After the week
- decide if you were successful or not
- discuss with others why it is often hard to protect the environment.

2 Think about one normal day in your life. During the day you probably used up several resources, caused quite a lot of pollution and may have tried to conserve the environment.

Draw and complete a table like the one below to show, 'One day in my life'. Some ideas have been added to the table to help you.

Summary

If resources are misused they can be used up or they may harm the environment. It is important that resources are used sensibly and the environment is protected for the future. This needs careful planning and management.

Resources which I used up	Pollution which I caused	How I tried to conserve the environment
◆ Clean water	◆ Dirty water after my shower	◆ Went to the bottle-bank
◆ Had fish and chips at lunchtime	◆ Left chip paper in school playground	◆ Put empty drink can in dustbin

Who cares for the environment?

One of the jobs of the British Government is to try and protect the countryside. Three Government bodies are:

- the Countryside Commission which looks after country parks and long distance footpaths
- the Forestry Commission which is mainly interested in coniferous forests
- the Nature Conservancy Council which has developed Nature Reserves.

However, there are also many voluntary groups of people (**conservationists**) who are concerned with protecting the environment. Some of these groups are named in diagram **A**. All of these groups have to rely upon donations of money to help them do their job.

A

Each group tends to concentrate upon one, and sometimes more, aspects of the environment. Some look after areas of **attractive countryside**, some look after **wildlife habitats** while others are more interested in **historic sites** (diagram **B**). They are all working to stop further damage to the environment.

B

Areas of attractive countryside
- Rivers
- Lakes
- Mountains
- Coasts
- Moors

Wildlife habitats
(homes of plants and animals)
- Woods
- Hedges
- Wetlands (marshes)

Historic sites
- Stately homes
- Castles
- Industrial museums

Activities

1 What do we mean by the following terms?

conservationist

attractive countryside

wildlife habitat

historic site

2 Sketch **C** shows several different environments which need special protection. These environments are areas of attractive countryside, wildlife habitats and historic sites. They have been numbered ① to ⑫.

a) Which three are likely to be looked after by Government bodies?

b) Which of the voluntary groups named in diagram **A** may look after each of the remaining nine environments?

① Rock crags – habitat for rare eagles

② Mountains with lake

③ Old mill with water wheel, now an industrial museum

④ Oak woodland

⑤ Good fishing river

⑥ Country park

⑦ Newly planted coniferous forest

⑧ Remains of old castle on attractive coast

⑨ Stately home

Old canal

Clean river

⑪ Wetland (marsh) for water birds

⑩ Nature reserve

Town

⑫ Dolphins

EXTRA

People in the town on sketch **C** like visiting the mountains and lake. They need a better road to make their journey easier and faster. Where would you build the road so that it did not upset any conservation group? Describe your route and say what problems there might be.

Summary

Some types of environment need special protection. These environments include areas of attractive countryside, wildlife habitats and historic sites. Some of these environments are looked after by Government bodies, while others are protected by voluntary conservation groups.

Why does wildlife need protecting?

Wildlife is always under threat from people. Some **species** (types) of plants, animals, birds and fish have already become **extinct**. Extinct means that there are no more of that species still living. Many other species of wildlife are said to be **endangered**. Unless something is done quickly to help and protect these endangered species they too will become extinct. Table **A** and the photos in **B** give examples of some endangered species, together with reasons why they have become endangered.

A

Examples of endangered species	Reasons for becoming endangered
Crocodiles and alligators	Skin is used for shoes, handbags and belts
Leopards, cheetahs and jaguars	Fur is used for clothes
Hawksbill turtles	Can no longer breed on beaches since these are full of tourists
Rhinos	Killed for their horns. A dagger with a rhino horn handle costs £10,000
Blue butterflies	Virtually extinct in the UK as their natural habitat has been destroyed
Whales and dolphins	Killed for food, caught in fishing nets
Elephants (photo **C**)	Killed for their ivory
Other endangered species include gorillas, giant pandas, tigers, parrots, orchids and many cacti plants.	

B

Elephants in Kenya – the problem

The long tusks of elephants are made of ivory. Ivory is taken from dead elephants and many have been killed for their tusks. Their trunks are often cut off to make the job of hacking out the tusks with axes easier. Most of the ivory from Kenya was sent to places like Hong Kong and Japan to be made into ornaments (photo **D**). As the world's trade and the price of ivory increased, more and more elephants were killed. Even when the Kenyan Government created the country's first national park in 1948, it did not stop the many poachers from killing elephants. Of the 111,000 elephants in Kenya in 1973, only 65,000 were left by 1981 and 19,000 in 1987. In fourteen years more than eight out of every ten elephants were killed. The elephant had become an endangered species.

Kenya needs it elephants. They, and other animals, are an important source of wealth to the country because they attract tourists (photo **F**). Many people come from overseas to go on safari, which means they can see wildlife in its natural habitat. Elephants are also useful to other wildlife in the area. They dig for water in dry areas, making it available to other species, they make tracks for smaller animals through thick vegetation and, on death, provide food for many predators for many weeks.

What has been done?

- President Moi of Kenya, a keen conservationist, has done much to stop the world trade in ivory.
- Conservation groups like WWF (World Wide Fund for Nature) raised money to help guard the elephant. They helped set up a new conservation group called CITES (Convention on International Trade in Endangered Species). This led in 1990 to a world ban on trading in ivory.
- Education within Kenyan schools and advertising on T-shirts (cartoon **E**) has helped to protect elephants.

By the mid-1990s, the number of elephants, especially in southern Africa, had begun to increase. Some scientists and politicians now even suggest that elephants can be treated as a 'crop', and surplus elephants 'harvested'. Income from the sale of ivory, skins and meat could help local communities and pay for conservation.

Activities

1 **a)** What is meant by 'endangered species'?
   b) Give **five** reasons why some species have become endangered.

2 Design **either** a poster **or** a T-shirt to remind people that ivory souvenirs will have cost an elephant its life.

3 Choose one endangered species. It might be one shown in the photos in **B** or another one that you know about. Explain why that species has become endangered. Give reasons why you think that it needs to be protected.

Summary

Many species of wildlife have become rare and are threatened with extinction. They need careful protection if they are to survive.

71

Why does the Antarctic need protecting?

The southern continent of Antarctica covers one tenth of the world's surface. Although larger than the continents of Europe and Australasia, it is a **wilderness**. It is called a wilderness because it is a desert of ice where nothing can grow and where nobody lives permanently. It is a place where the wind can reach 300 km per hour (190 m.p.h.), temperatures can fall below minus 50°C and the depth of ice can exceed 4,500 metres. Where the ice reaches the coast it forms tall ice cliffs. In time, huge blocks of ice break off to form icebergs (photo **A**).

Antarctica is the most unspoilt region on Earth. It is still mainly a natural environment free from pollution – but for how long? It is a continent with valuable resources – but how can it be protected?

A

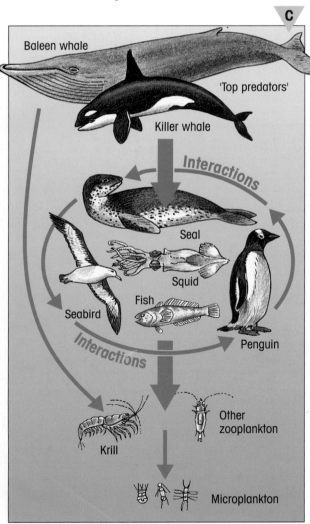

C

Baleen whale

'Top predators'

Killer whale

Interactions

Seal

Squid

Fish

Seabird

Penguin

Interactions

Krill

Other zooplankton

Microplankton

What are the Antarctic's resources?

The relatively few species of **wildlife** are, however, found in large numbers. All wildlife depends upon plankton and krill which thrive in the polar sea. Plankton is a minute plant which is eaten by the small shrimp-like krill. Krill provide the food for the majority of seabirds, fish, penguins, squid, seals and whales (photo **B** and diagram **C**). Several countries fish the Southern Ocean for krill, squid and fin fish. Although Antarctica contains mineral deposits, no-one has yet suggested that they could be exploited for economic gain.

B

Why does the Antarctic need protecting?

Antarctica needs protecting because it is a fragile environment where even small amounts of damage can have serious effects on the surroundings and, in particular, wildlife. Some past and present concerns include:

● Pollution around scientific bases in the early days of Antarctic exploration.
● Until recently, overfishing, particularly of krill and whales. See diagram **C** for the effects of overfishing.
● New problems caused by the recent increase of tourism (up to 10,000 visitors a year).

D Satellite image of Antarctica

Southern Ocean

Weddell Sea

Antarctic Circle

South Pole

International scientific stations

How can the Antarctic be protected?

Since the mid 1980s there has been a growing international awareness of the need to preserve Antarctica. Much progress has been made in recent years. The Protocol on Environmental Protection (1991), for example, aims to make the Antarctic 'a natural reserve devoted to peace and science'.

The Protocol is supported by groups such as Greenpeace and WWF and once it is signed by all 26 active Antarctic nations, will help to protect the entire continent as well as the seas around it. To date, 22 nations have signed the agreement, including the UK. Some ways of protecting the Antarctic are shown in **E**.

E

New runways for aircraft reduce costs and help scientists reach study sites more easily.

Strict marine pollution controls stop the discharge of fuel from ships.

Fishing has to be sustainable.

Some sewage can be released into the sea to provide food for certain birds.

All waste such as empty tins, bottles and plastic must be removed.

The Southern Ocean has been made a whale sanctuary. Mining is banned for 50 years.

Scientists can study global warming, sea level changes and ozone depletion.

Areas of special scientific interest are carefully managed and plants and animals protected.

Visitors are requested not to tread on vegetation and to keep their distance from wildlife.

Krill fishing is now regulated and its importance in the ecosystem is recognised.

Activities

1 Copy out and complete a Fact File on Antarctica using the following table.

Climate	Scenery	Sea resources	Land resources

2 a) What is krill?
   b) Why is it important to the Antarctic?
   c) Why is krill being threatened?

3 Draw a star diagram to show at least four reasons why the Antarctic needs protecting.

4 From diagram **E** above:
   a) Give four ways of protecting the sea environment.
   b) Give four ways of protecting the land environment.
   c) Give two ways of supporting scientific research.

Summary

The Antarctic has many very useful resources. It is also one of the few environments not yet spoilt by people. People have to choose which is more important – to use these resources, or to protect the environment.

What are non-renewable and renewable resources?

It is possible to divide the world's natural resources into two groups.

1 **Non-renewable** resources are those which can only be used once. Coal, for example, can only be burnt once. In time these resources will run out.

2 **Renewable** resources can be used over and over again.
- Some, like the sun and the wind, will never run out.
- Others can only be used again if they are **recycled** (e.g. paper) or if they are not misused by people (e.g. soil).

Energy resources

We all need energy to help us to work and to play. If we work or play hard we give off heat and use up energy. We have to eat and drink to replace this lost energy. Energy in nature also does work and can give off heat. Coal, for example, can be used to work machines and to heat water.

Sketch **A** shows five main types of **non-renewable** energy resources. These have, so far, been easy and quite cheap to use. Coal, oil and natural gas are called **fossil fuels** because they come from the remains (fossils) of plants and animals. As each of these are used to produce energy they all create a lot of pollution (pages 78–79). They are also causing changes in the world's climate.

A

Oil is used for heating, lighting, transport and to produce electricity

Natural gas is used for heating and to produce electricity

Nuclear energy uses a mineral called uranium to produce electricity

Wood is often the only source of energy in countries which do not have a lot of money

Coal is used for heating and to produce electricity

Sketch **B** shows six main types of **renewable** energy resources. These, in comparison with non-renewable types, are more difficult and expensive to use. However, where they can be used they cause far less pollution.

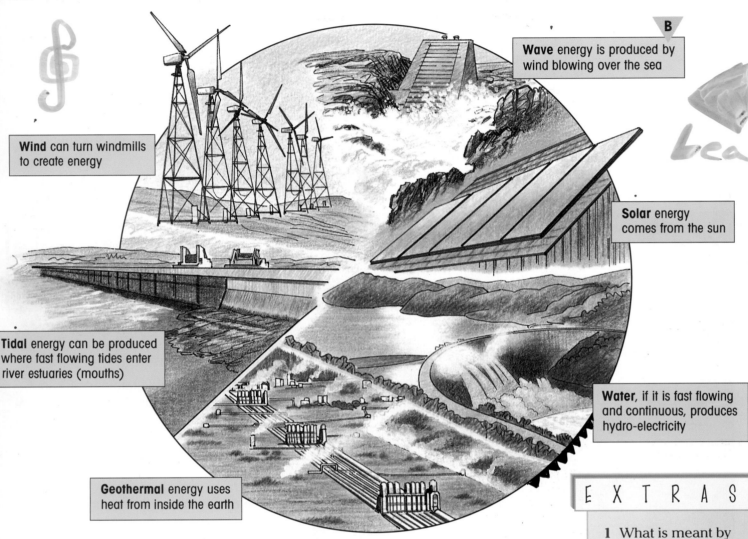

Wind can turn windmills to create energy

Wave energy is produced by wind blowing over the sea

Solar energy comes from the sun

Tidal energy can be produced where fast flowing tides enter river estuaries (mouths)

Water, if it is fast flowing and continuous, produces hydro-electricity

Geothermal energy uses heat from inside the earth

B

Activities

1 Make a copy of table **C**. Complete it by choosing the correct words from the following list:

- ◆ can only be used once
- ◆ can be used over and over again
- ◆ costs a lot to produce
- ◆ quite cheap to produce
- ◆ causes much pollution
- ◆ causes little pollution

C

Non-renewable	Renewable

2 Complete the following sentences.
   a) Three fossil fuels which give energy are _____, _____ and _____.
   b) Three types of energy using water are _____, _____ and _____.
   c) A hilly place with a wet and windy climate can produce _____ and _____ energy.
   d) A coastal place with a lot of sun and wind can produce _____, _____ and _____ energy.
   e) Uranium gives _____ energy.
   f) Heat from the earth gives _____ energy.

Summary

Natural resources can be divided into non-renewable and renewable resources. Non-renewable resources, which can only be used once, are usually cheaper to use but cause more pollution.

E X T R A S

1 What is meant by 'recycling'?

2 List items which you use in a normal day which are, or could be, recycled.

Oil and the environment

Exploitation is a term which you should try to understand. It is when we use or develop something for our own benefit. It means using something selfishly without thinking about how it affects other people or the environment. In this section we will see how our use of oil to make our lives easier and more pleasant can also harm the environment.

The use of any type of energy causes some pollution. The exploitation of fossil fuels, such as oil, can cause much pollution. This means that a lot of careful planning and management is necessary if we are to make the most of fossil fuels while at the same time protecting the environment.

A Stages in the exploitation of oil

1 Exploration for new oil fields either under the ground or the sea

2 Oil is reached by drilling into the ground or under the sea

3 Oil is moved by pipeline or oil tanker to an oil refinery

4 Oil is stored until it is needed

5 At the refinery the oil is turned into petrol for cars or refined for use in power stations

B

C

How can the exploitation of oil harm the environment?

Each stage in the exploitation of oil can threaten the environment in different ways.

On land – large areas have to be cleared when drilling for oil, for laying pipelines and building refineries and terminals (photo **B**). This can:

- destroy natural vegetation and wildlife habitats
- be an eyesore, especially if the area has attractive scenery
- cause noise when drilling for oil and when the refinery is working
- cause fumes to be released into the air when the oil is being refined.

At sea – most of Britain's oil is found under the North Sea or is imported from overseas. It is taken to refineries, which are found in ports, by pipeline or oil tanker.

- Drilling rigs in the North Sea are ugly and can be a hazard to shipping.
- If pipelines break or oil tankers run aground oil can be spilled. This can kill wildlife and pollute beaches (photo **C**).
- If there is an explosion on a drilling rig or oil tanker then serious fires can occur, endangering lives (photo **D**). Smoke causes air pollution (photo **E**).

D

E

F How can oil companies protect the environment?

1 | Before drilling begins a study is made of wildlife.

2 | Routes for pipelines and oil tankers are chosen carefully so as to avoid wildlife habitats and attractive scenery.

3 | Once pipelines are laid the ground is restored.

4 | Drilling sites on land are lined with concrete. Sites at sea are surrounded by booms to trap any oil spills.

5 | Refineries are screened behind trees. They can be painted green or dark brown.

6 | Muffles are put on machines to reduce noise.

7 | When the oil is used up, the land is returned to its original use.

Activities

1 Write out the meaning of *exploitation*.

2 a) Show the five stages of oil exploitation by drawing diagram **G** and putting the boxes in the correct order.
b) Link your boxes by arrows.

3 a) Write short newspaper headlines like the ones in **H** to show five more ways by which the exploitation of oil can harm the environment.

G

4 — Storage

1 — Exploration

5 — Refining

2 — Drilling

3 — Transport

b) For two of your headings write short newspaper articles to describe what happened.

H

Oilslick spoils golden sands

Oil refinery noise keeps locals away

E X T R A

Find out at least six different uses of oil.

Summary The exploitation of any type of energy can damage the environment. Most damage is done by fossil fuels such as oil. However, with careful planning and management the damage can be kept to a minimum.

Electricity and the environment

Most of Britain's electricity is produced in **thermal power stations** (photo **A**). Thermal power is when electricity is produced by heat. Heat is obtained by burning coal and oil. These are two non-renewable fossil fuels (page 74).

Diagram **B** shows a simplified version of what happens in a thermal power station that uses coal. Large amounts of coal are needed to heat water, and turn it into steam. Steam is then used to turn, or drive, a turbine. As the turbine turns, or rotates, it turns another machine called a generator. It is the generator which produces electricity. Later, large amounts of water are used to cool the steam and to condense it back into water. This is done in large cooling towers (photos **A** and **C**).

Can you imagine living without electricity? In what ways does it make our lives easier and more pleasant? Unfortunately, the production of electricity in thermal power stations can seriously harm and pollute our environment. Four types of pollution are labelled ① to ④ on diagram **B**.

A

When coal or oil is burnt to heat water, waste gases are given off. These gases are released into the air from tall chimneys (photo **C**). Two of these gases are very harmful. One is sulphur dioxide, which causes **acid rain** and kills trees and fish. The other is carbon dioxide, which is causing world temperatures to rise. This is called **global warming** (diagram **D**).

①

The buildings, chimneys and cooling towers are unsightly and take up large amounts of land. The pylons that support wires through which electricity is sent to all parts of Britain are also unsightly.

②

B

Coal (or oil)

Water

Waste gases given off

Pylons hold cables which carry electricity to rest of UK

Water heated in boiler

Steam, at high pressure, is used to turn turbine

Turbine turns a generator to give electricity

Steam is turned back into water in cooling tower

Once used, the coal leaves large amounts of waste ash.

③

Some water is released from the cooling towers back into rivers. As this water is warm, it can kill fish.

④

How can pollution be reduced?

The electricity companies are introducing a way of stopping sulphur dioxide from being released into the air. It is hoped that if limestone is added then it can absorb 90 per cent of the gas. Although this will greatly reduce the effects of acid rain, it will also increase the amount of limestone which has to be quarried. Quarrying often takes place in areas of attractive countryside and can itself spoil the environment (page 25).

Conservation groups favour the use of renewable types of energy to produce electricity (page 75). As yet, these alternative methods are neither as cheap nor as easy to use as fossil fuels. Although wind power may be used by early next century, other forms of power may have to wait until cheaper ways of using them are found or governments become more concerned about protecting the environment.

Several things can be done to reduce the harm done to the environment, but they all cost a lot of money. To pay for these things means putting up the price of electricity. Our problem is that we want cheap electricity and a clean environment. At present we have to choose between them.

C

D

① Earth is heated by the sun during the day.

② Earth loses heat at night. Some heat kept in by a layer of gases in the atmosphere.

③ Thermal power stations burn fossil fuels and release carbon dioxide.

④ Carbon dioxide increases the layer of gases.

⑤ Thicker layer of gases acts as a blanket and prevents heat loss. The earth gets hotter.

Sun

Activities

1 a) What is a thermal power station?
  b) Name **two** fossil fuels used in thermal power stations.

2 Photo **A** and diagram **B** show how electricity is produced in a thermal power station. In description **E** the key words have been missed out although their first letters have been given. Copy out the description and fill in the missing words.

3 Describe how the production of electricity can harm the
  a) air
  b) water and
  c) landscape (scenery).

4 Which of the two opinions given in cartoon **F** do you think is more important? Give reasons for your answer.

E

How e_____ is produced in a thermal power station

The power station needs a large area of f_____ land. It needs plenty of c____ to heat w____ to make s____. Waste g____ from the coal are released into the a_____. The steam turns a t____ which turns a g_____ which produces e____. The steam is cooled by water in a c____ t____. Warm water may be released into r____.

F

It is better to have cheap electricity than to worry about the environment.

The protection of the environment is much more important than cheap electricity.

Summary Using coal and oil are the easiest and cheapest ways to produce electricity, but they also cause the most pollution.

New technology and the oil industry

Many industrialised countries in the world have come to rely on oil. They need it for transport, energy and heating. Oil is a non-renewable resource, and more and more countries use oil. The cheapest sources, and the easiest to use, have been exhausted. Oil is getting more expensive and harder to find and exploit. This means that oil companies have had to improve their **technology**. Technology is when industry finds new ways of doing things and uses new equipment and materials. In the oil industry, improved technology has been needed to find new supplies of oil, then to drill, move and refine that oil.

Map **A** shows where most of the world's oil is found. Oil is often found:
● in areas where the climate and relief make exploration and drilling very difficult (photos **C**, **D** and **E**)
● a long way from the countries that use most of the oil – this makes transport both difficult and expensive (photo **B**).

B

Where oil has to go a long way, it can be carried by pipes since it is a liquid

Frozen ground in Alaska. New ways of drilling where needed

C

A

Alaska

USA

Mexico

Venezuela

Peru

Western Europe

Saudi Arabia

Algeria

Libya

Middle East

Nigeria

Japan

Indonesia

Hot, dry deserts. Oil is sent to coast by pipeline and then overseas by large oil tankers

D

E

Tropical rainforests. Difficult to explore, drill and to move oil

Key

⸻ Large oil tanker route

Japan

Places needing oil

DESERTS STRESSED
deserts

The North Sea

Britain uses a lot of oil. At first it came from overseas countries. In the 1960s oil companies began to look for oil under the North Sea. They were able to do this because they developed new technology in underwater **exploration**. When oil was found in 1970 new ways had to be found to **drill** for the oil and then **transport** it to the coast. Improved technology has helped oil companies to drill under the North Sea and to bring oil ashore (diagram **F**).

Once ashore oil cannot be used until it has been refined. Refining gets rid of waste products. It also gives different types of oil which are needed for different purposes.

F

Helipad Helicopters can bring in daily supplies of food and mail. Needed in case of emergencies (storms and illness).

Living quarters Many people work on the rig for several weeks at a time.

The North Sea is between 80 and 180 metres in depth.

Pipelines had to be laid on a very uneven seabed. Checks have to be made to make sure there are no breaks or oil spillages.

To coast

Drilling derrick

Crane

Lifeboat

Flare boom for burning waste gases.

Control room Full of computers and modern information technology.

Ways had to be found to close the well in case of fire or explosions.

Oil-rig supported on long legs. New technology needed to keep the rig upright in severe storms and huge waves.

The height of some well-known landmarks

100 metres
60
20

An oil-rig 100–130 m

St Paul's Cathedral 111 m

Nelson's Column 52 m

Electricity pylon 50 m

English oak tree

Future exploration and drilling will be in deeper, stormier seas and further from the coast. This will need new technology.

Activities

1 What is meant by the word 'technology'?

2 Using map **A**, photos **B**, **C**, **D** and **E** and diagram **F**, complete the following sentences by naming the correct places.

3 **a)** List **five** problems which had to be overcome before Britain could get oil from under the North Sea.
   b) Describe how new technology has overcome any **two** of those problems.

◆ Drilling is difficult due to the cold in _____.

◆ Drilling is difficult as it is very hot and dry in _____.

◆ Drilling is difficult in the rainforests in _____ and _____.

◆ Drilling is difficult where the oil is found under the _____ Sea and the Gulf of M_____.

◆ Oil has to be sent by large oil tankers from _____ and _____.

◆ Oil has to be moved by pipeline in _____.

◆ Two places which get oil by tanker are _____ and _____.

Summary

The development of new technology has helped the oil industry to find new sources of oil, and then to drill, transport and refine that oil.

The environment enquiry

Many environments need special protection and are looked after by government bodies or voluntary organisations. **The Wildlife Trusts** form the largest conservation group in the UK. The Trusts protect wildlife in towns and the countryside and rely upon donations of money to help do their job.

The Trusts help protect and conserve wildlife through planning and management. They:
- promote better access to wildlife areas
- work with schools and local communities
- provide information and organise events and clubs
- encourage a sustainable approach to wildlife conservation
- carry out improvements to nature reserves.

A

More information on the Wildlife Trusts can be found on their website at: www.wildlifetrusts.org

In this enquiry, you are a member of a team working for one of the Wildlife Trusts and have been given the task of improving a small nature reserve like the one in map **A** above. Your three main aims are:
- to improve facilities so that wildlife is protected and encouraged
- to improve public access within the reserve
- to improve visitor facilities and help promote enjoyment and understanding for the public.

The Heritage Lottery Fund has promised £25,000 towards the work, and a further £5,000 has been collected from Wildlife Trust members.

It will be best if you can work with a partner or in a small group. You will then be able to share views and discuss ideas with each other.

How can planning and management help protect the environment?

1 Look carefully at the suggestions on the next page and discuss how best to spend the money.

2 Draw up a table to show all the suggestions. Decide which you will use and how much will be spent on each one. Complete your table.

3 Write a report for the Project Director giving details of your plan. In your report describe what you propose to do and explain how each of your suggestions will help improve the reserve. Link your explanations to the three main aims.

4 Draw a poster encouraging people to visit your improved nature reserve.

B

£200 pays for 10 **red squirrel feeders.**

£200 pays for 20 **nest boxes** for fixing to trees.

Thorney Mere

£100 will print 5,000 **wildlife trail leaflets.**

£100 will fund a **gate for disabled visitors.**

£2 will plant **a tree or shrub**: 1,000 trees will turn an area 100 x 100 metres into woodland.

£5,000 pays for 100 metres of **board-walk** in muddy, less accessible areas.

A medium-sized **hide for wildlife watching** costs about £5,000.

Should all paths be boardwalk, or just to the first viewpoint?

Do we save money for trees, squirrel feeders or nest boxes?

Do we put hides at all viewpoints?

How can we encourage visitors?

Improvements to the Visitor Centre will cost about £5,000 per room.

£50 pays for an after-school **environmental club meeting** or one **school visit.**

Now where's the best place to live?

What affects where we live?

Not only is the distribution of population uneven in Britain, but it is uneven throughout the world. There are now over 5,000 million people in the world yet most of them live on only a third of the land surface. Like Britain, some areas are very crowded and others are almost empty.

There are many reasons for this. People do not like to live in places which are too wet or too dry, too hot or too cold. Nor do they like places that are mountainous, lack vegetation, are densely forested or liable to flood. People prefer pleasant places in which to live. They want to be able to earn money by working and have food available

through farming or from shops. They like to be near to other people and have things to do and places to go.

Factors that discourage people from settling in an area are called **negative factors**. Factors that encourage people to live in an area are called **positive factors**. Some of these are shown in the photos below and in diagram **G** on the next page.

Look carefully at the photos and for each one in turn try to work out why it is likely to be either a densely populated area or a sparsely populated area.

A Himalayan Mountains

B Amazon Forest

C Western Europe

D Sahara Desert

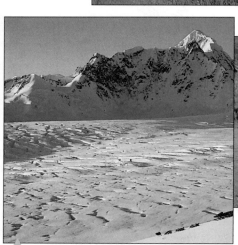

E Polar regions – Antarctica

F Bangladesh

G

NEGATIVE FACTORS
(sparse population)
- Very cold
- Steep slopes
- Poor soils
- Dense forest
- Very hot
- Very dry
- Poor water supply
- Few raw materials
- Little industry
- Not many jobs

POSITIVE FACTORS
(dense population)
- Pleasant climate
- Gentle slopes
- Good soils
- Open grassland
- Lowland
- Food supply
- Water supply
- Raw materials
- Industry and jobs
- Good communications

Activities

1 a) Which one of the photos **A** to **F** does this list of words and phrases best describe:
steep slopes • snowy • icy • very cold • mountainous • no soil • no industry • very few people?

b) Which of these could be used to describe photo **F**:
hot • cold • wet • dry • steep • level • poor soils • good farming • factory work • many people • sparse population?

c) Imagine that you are passing through the desert in photo **D**. Make a list of words and phrases to describe what it would be like. Try to give at least **eight** different things.

2 Draw table **H** and put the following into the correct columns:

H

Sparsely populated (negative factors)	Densely populated (positive factors)
🚶 🚶 🚶	👥👥👥👥👥👥👥👥👥👥👥

3 Give **two** reasons why few people live in
a) mountain areas
b) desert areas.

E X T R A

Is the place where you live crowded or sparsely populated? What are the reasons for this? List the factors from diagram **G** which affect your area. Add any others that you think are important.

flat land   mountains   dense forest   lowland   deserts
open grassland   deep, rich soils   unreliable water supply   poor farming
good farming   thin, poor soils   job opportunities

Summary

The way people are spread across the world is affected by many different things. These include relief, climate, vegetation, water supply, raw materials and employment opportunities.

Where do we live?

The photo-map below is quite remarkable. It is made up from more than 37 million satellite images carefully put together to give a picture of the world. The red dots have been added to show the distribution of population. Look carefully and you can see many of the world's major features. The cold **polar regions** show up as white. The densely forested parts of South America and Africa are a lush green. The areas that are dry and lacking vegetation are shades of brown. Can you see the great mountain ranges? They show up as patches or streaks of white.

The map also confirms how unevenly people are spread over the world. Vast areas have hardly any people living in them whilst other areas seem to be very crowded. Try to name some of the emptiest places. Places with a lot of people include parts of Western Europe, India, China and Japan. Where else in the world does the photo-map show that there are a lot of people?

Photos of the six areas described below are shown on page 86.

A

Amazon Forest
Too hot and wet for people.
Dense forest makes communications and settlement difficult.
Sparsely populated.

Western Europe
Low-lying and gently sloping.
Pleasant climate.
Good water supply and soil for farming.
Easy communications and many resources for industry.
Densely populated.

Himalayan Mountains
Too cold for people.
Steep slopes are bad for communications and settlement.
Poor, thin soil unsuitable for crops.
Sparsely populated.

Polar regions – Antarctica
Too cold for people.
No soil for crops.
Snow and ice make communications and settlement very difficult.
Sparsely populated.

Sahara Desert
Too hot and dry for people.
Too dry and too little soil for crops to grow.
Sand makes communications difficult.
Sparsely populated.

Bangladesh
Low-lying and flat.
Rich, fertile soil. Hot and wet.
Ideal farming conditions.
Densely populated.

Cities are very popular places in which to live. They can provide housing, jobs, education, medical care and a better chance of getting on and enjoying life. More than half the world's population now live in cities and the number is increasing all the time.

The fastest growing cities tend to be in the poorer countries. Here, the urban population is expected to double in the next ten years. This will produce some very large cities.

One of these, Mexico City, is expected to overtake Tokyo, and become the largest city in the world by the year 2005. By then it will have a population of more than 33 million. At present its size is increasing by over half a million people a year. That is the same as all the inhabitants of Liverpool or Edinburgh suddenly arriving in Mexico City in a single year. Think of the problems that such a rapid increase must cause.

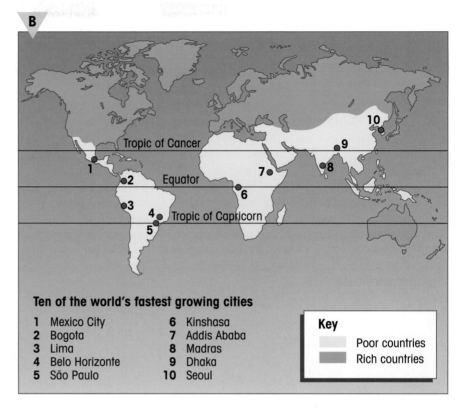

B

Tropic of Cancer
Equator
Tropic of Capricorn

Ten of the world's fastest growing cities

1	Mexico City	6	Kinshasa
2	Bogota	7	Addis Ababa
3	Lima	8	Madras
4	Belo Horizonte	9	Dhaka
5	São Paulo	10	Seoul

Key

Poor countries
Rich countries

Activities

1 Copy and complete the sentences below using the following words:

densely   uneven   sparsely   deserts   polar regions

a) The distribution of population over the world is _____.
b) The areas with the fewest people are the dense forests, _____ and _____.
c) Mountainous areas are _____ populated.
d) Areas with good resources and industry are _____ populated.

2 Give named examples of:
a) four densely populated areas
b) six sparsely populated areas.

3 Which of the fastest growing cities are in:
a) South America
b) Africa
c) Asia?

4 Of the eight statements given below, three are correct. Write out the correct ones. The ten fastest growing cities are
● in poor countries.
● in rich countries.
● mainly in polar regions.
● mainly between the tropics.
● on the coast.
● spread all over the world.
● in one continent.
● in South America, Africa and Asia.

5 Copy star diagram **C** and complete your diagram to show six reasons why people like to live in cities.

EXTRAS

1 Use an atlas to name a country for each of the fastest growing cities in map **B**.
2 With help from an atlas, try to find out why central Australia is sparsely populated and east and south-west USA are densely populated.

C

Why cities are popular

Summary

People are not spread evenly over the world. Some of the most crowded places are in China, India, parts of Western Europe, and some areas of Africa and the USA. More and more people in the world are living in cities.

How does population change?

The population of the world is increasing very quickly. Experts have worked out that every hour there are an extra 8,000 people living on our planet. That is an increase of about 2 people every second or enough people to fill a city the size of Birmingham in about a week. In 1987 the world's population passed the 5,000 million mark and by the year 2000 it had risen to over 6,000 million. This increase in population is now so fast that it is often described as a **population explosion**.

A major world problem is how to feed, clothe, house, educate, provide jobs and care for this rapidly increasing population.

Graph **A** shows the changes in world population since the year 1100. Notice how the population increase is not even. Until one hundred or two hundred years ago the population growth was actually very slow. Only in recent times has there been a real 'explosion'.

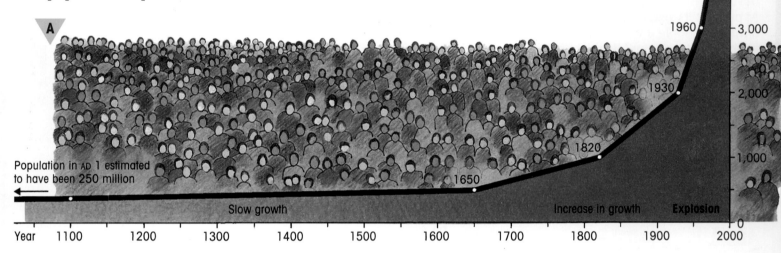

A

Millions of people

6,000

1987 — 5,000

1974 — 4,000

1960 — 3,000

1930

2,000

1820

1,000

1650

Population in AD 1 estimated to have been 250 million

Slow growth   Increase in growth   **Explosion**

0

Year 1100   1200   1300   1400   1500   1600   1700   1800   1900   2000

Population increases when the number of babies being born is greater than the number of people dying. The number of babies being born each year is called the **birth rate**. The number of people who die each year is called the **death rate**. Birth rates and death rates are measured as the number of births and deaths for each 1,000 of the population. The speed at which the population increases is called the **population growth rate**. Diagrams **B**, **C** and **D** show how the balance between births and deaths affects the population growth.

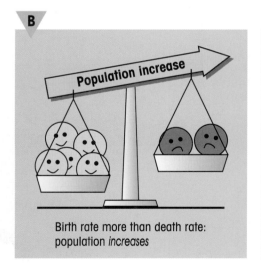

B

Population increase

Birth rate more than death rate: population *increases*

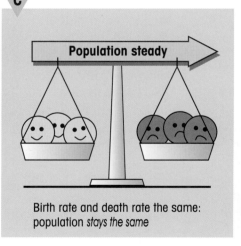

C

Population steady

Birth rate and death rate the same: population *stays the same*

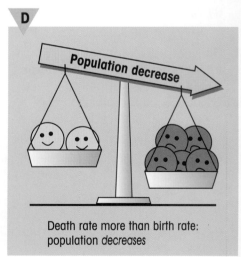

D

Population decrease

Death rate more than birth rate: population *decreases*

The population growth rate is not the same for all countries. In some, like Britain, the difference between birth and death rates is small so the population is changing only very slowly. In other countries, like Bangladesh, there are big differences between birth and death rates so the population is increasing rapidly.

E

Country	Birth rate	Death rate	Natural increase
Bangladesh	41	14	27
Brazil	26	8	18
China	21	7	14
France	13	10	3
India	31	10	21
Italy	11	10	1
Japan	12	8	4
Mexico	27	5	22
UK	14	12	2
USA	14	9	5

(1994)

- Figures given per 1,000 people.
- Poorer countries are shaded yellow.
- **Natural increase** is the difference between birth and death rates.

Table **E** shows birth and death rates for some countries. Remember, the greater the difference between births and deaths, the larger the population change will be.

F Things that can affect birth and death rates

Food shortages

New hospitals

Good harvest

Poor health care

Improved water supply

War

Children needed to help with work

Birth control available

Traditions for larger families

Activities

1 a) When did the world's population reach 1,000 million?

b) How long did it take to double to 2,000 million?

c) How long did it take to double again to 4,000 million?

E X T R A S

1 Draw table **H** below and from diagram **F** sort the things that affect birth rates and death rates into the correct columns.

H

Birth rate		Death rate	
High	Low	High	Low

2 Suggest **three** reasons why people in the UK may be more likely to live longer than people in poorer countries.

2 Describe the increase in world population shown in graph **A**.

3 a) Write a sentence to explain what each of the following terms means.
- Birth rate
- Death rate
- Population growth rate

b) Why is 'explosion' a good description of population changes since 1950?

4 Copy and complete table **G** below by writing **increase**, **same** or **decrease** in the last column.

G

Births	Deaths	Population change
→	→	
→	↗	
→	↓	
→	↗	

5 a) List the countries from table **E** by the size of their natural increase. Put the one with the greatest increase first.

b) What do you notice about the richer and the poorer countries?

Summary

The world's population is increasing at a very rapid rate. Growth is very much faster in the poorer countries than in the richer ones. Population changes in a country depend mainly on the birth and death rates.

What is migration?

Mexico City is one of the largest cities in the world. It is also one of the fastest growing. This is partly because of natural increase but mainly because like most cities, it acts like a magnet and attracts people from other places to live there.

People who move from one place to another to live or work are called **migrants**. They have a big effect on populations because they increase the numbers and can alter the 'mix' of people who are living in a place.

Graph **A** shows how quickly Mexico City has grown since 1940. The photos in **C** show some people who have migrated to Mexico City. Notice how different they look and what varied backgrounds they have. Their comments may help to explain some of the reasons why people migrate.

A **Population of Mexico City**

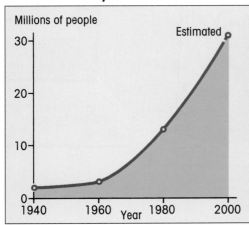

Millions of people

Estimated

30

20

10

0

1940 · 1960 · 1980 · 2000
Year

B Mexico City

C

Pedro

I'm from a village down on the coast and was injured in an accident. My family live in Mexico City so I've come to join them. I hope to get good medical care here.

Maria

I went to college in Acapulco but I'm ambitious and think that I'll have a better chance of getting a good job and enjoying life in Mexico's capital city.

Janine

I've just qualified as a nurse in New York. I came to Mexico City so that I could help people who are less well off than myself.

Carlos

I came here from Spain. My company in Madrid sent me to Mexico City some years ago and I like it so much that I'm going to stay.

Zina

I've lived here all my life but I'm descended from slaves who were brought across from Africa many years ago.

Taxa

I was brought up in a small Indian village in the mountains. I had very little future there because conditions were primitive and there were no proper jobs or education.

Migration is when people move home. The movement may be just around the corner to a better house. It may be from one part of the country to another in search of a job. It might be from one country to another for a different way of life. For many people country areas have very little to offer so they move to the towns and cities. This is called **rural-to-urban migration**. For other people a move to a different country holds many attractions. This is called **international migration**.

People migrate for two reasons. Firstly, they may wish to get away from things that they do not like. These are called **push factors** and include a shortage of jobs and poor living conditions. Secondly, people are attracted to things that they do like. These are called **pull factors** and include pleasant surroundings and good medical care.

D

PUSH FACTORS →

- Political fears
- Not enough jobs
- Few opportunities
- Natural disasters
- Wars
- Unhappy life
- Shortage of food

PULL FACTORS →

Hope for
- Better way of life
- Chances of a job
- Improved living conditions
- Education
- Better housing
- Medical care
- Family links

Activities

1 What do each of these terms mean?
- Migration
- Rural-to-urban migration
- International migration

2 a) Copy and complete bar graph **E** to show population growth in Mexico City.
b) Describe the increase in Mexico City's population since 1940. Use your graph and graph **A** to help you. Give actual figures.
c) Suggest reasons for this growth.

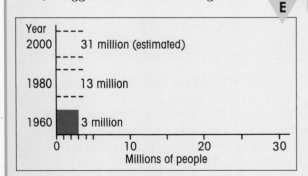

E

Year		
2000	31 million (estimated)	
1980	13 million	
1960	3 million	

0   10   20   30
Millions of people

3 a) What is a push factor? Give two examples.
b) What is a pull factor? Give two examples.

4 Copy table **F** and use it to explain why the people in **C** migrated to Mexico City.

F

	Push factor	Pull factor
Pedro		
Janine		
Zina		
Maria		
Carlos		
Taxa		

5 Imagine you are a migrant like Taxa in **C**.
a) You have just arrived in Mexico City. Describe your first few days there. Think about getting a job, food, shelter, making friends . . .
b) You left your village because of poor conditions there. What attracted you to the city?

Summary   Migration is the movement of people from one place to another. This movement may be the result of push and pull factors. The migration of people affects population size and the variety of different people in a place.

93

Why migrate to America?

The United States has much to offer migrants. It is a place with many opportunities, high standards of living, and an attractive way of life. It is one of the wealthiest places in the world, jobs are readily available, education is good and health care is excellent. All these things put together are sometimes called the 'American Dream' – a vision of freedom, opportunity and good living which is available for all.

For people living in the world's poorer countries, the USA is very attractive. Since 1940 many Mexicans have migrated northwards into the USA. They seek the 'American Dream' but most of all they go in search of work and the chance to earn money. They hope to rid themselves of the poverty and unemployment of Mexico and replace that with what they hope will be the wealth and opportunity of the USA.

A

Most Mexicans settle in California or Texas. Some cross the border legally but perhaps as many as two million a year cross without permission. Many Mexicans now live permanently in the USA but some stay there only on a temporary basis. Some **temporary migrants** take jobs that are **seasonal** and when the work is finished they return to Mexico. Others cross the border every day to work then return home at night. These people are called **migrant workers**.

Migrant workers do all kinds of work. Many work on large farms and in food processing factories. Others work in the cities where they often gain employment on construction projects, and in hotels and restaurants. Most do unskilled and low paid work but even in those occupations they can earn more in a month than they could in a full year in Mexico.

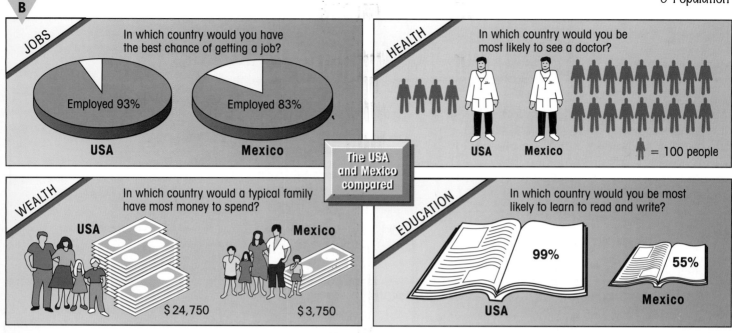

B

JOBS — In which country would you have the best chance of getting a job?

Employed 93% — **USA**

Employed 83% — **Mexico**

HEALTH — In which country would you be most likely to see a doctor?

USA   Mexico   👤 = 100 people

The USA and Mexico compared

WEALTH — In which country would a typical family have most money to spend?

USA $24,750   Mexico $3,750

EDUCATION — In which country would you be most likely to learn to read and write?

99% USA   55% Mexico

Activities

1 Copy diagram **C** and complete it to show **six** things that make up the 'American Dream'.

C

The American Dream

2 **a)** Copy and complete table **D** below using information from diagram **B**.
b) Explain why Mexicans are keen to migrate to the USA.

D

	USA	Mexico
Unemployment		
People per doctor		
Family income		
School attendance		

3 Diagram **E** shows how much a sewing machinist earns each week in the garment making trade.
a) Why do Mexicans like working in the USA?
b) Why do Americans like to employ Mexicans?
c) How does Mexican migrant labour help America to be prosperous?

4 On the right is a list of jobs that Mexican migrants do. Sort the jobs under the headings:

waitress • cook • nurse • fruit picker • electrician • farm labourer • rubbish collector • sewing machinist • petrol station attendant • construction worker

Low paid	Seasonal	Skilful

E X T R A S

1 Imagine that you are to migrate to America. What would you like most about the place if you were
a) a 12-year-old child
b) a parent with three children?

2 Draw a poster showing the advantages of living in the USA rather than in Mexico.

E

Mexico **$15**   Migrant in USA **$150**   US average **$300**

Summary

Migrants usually move from poor places to the nearest rich place. Many Mexicans migrate to their nearest neighbour, the USA. They move in the hope of gaining employment and a better chance in life.

What are the effects of migration?

There are many effects of migration. Some are good and some are bad. Some affect the migrant and others affect the place they have moved from and the place they move to. Look at sketches **B** and **C**, which show some of these effects.

A

B   Migration – the good…and the bad

> It's great here…we love it! Jose got a job straight away in a clothing factory. We have a small flat and the children are at a local school. We are all making progress with the language and have already made lots of friends. Migration was a good move for us…we are really very happy.

The Sanchez family

> I wish we had never left Mexico. We can't speak the language and have had great difficulty getting work and making friends. It's been hard finding a reasonable place to live because we have so little money and people just don't seem to want to help us. Migration has made us homesick and very unhappy.

The Pancho family

> I think the Mexicans are great. I can't afford to pay high wages but the Mexicans seem to be happy on low pay so that's good for my business and I'm happy to employ them. I think we should encourage Mexicans to live in America because they do jobs that we don't like and they are good for our economy

Eddie Ingle, restaurant owner

> I'm sick of these Mexicans coming into our country. They take our jobs, live in our houses and try to change our cities to suit their way of life. I don't have a job and I really don't think it's fair that a foreigner should get work before me.

Brad Bradley, unemployed

Activities

1 a) Give **five** reasons why the Sanchez family are pleased they migrated to America.

b) Give **five** reasons why the Pancho family are unhappy after migrating to America.

2 In the spiral **D** there are five effects of migration. Find them by starting at the centre and working outwards. Sort the effects into **Good** and **Bad**.

3 Write out the following statements that are **true**.
Migrant workers
- stop local people getting jobs.
- all live in California.
- help keep factories open.
- have large families.
- work long hours.
- change the way of life.

4 Suggest reasons for the headlines in **E**. Answer in the form of a short newspaper article for each one.

D

Y	R	A	C	I	A	L	P	R	O
T	F	J	O	B	S	C	H	E	B
I	O	O	N	A	R	E	O	A	L
R	S	I	F	E	C	T	V	P	E
E	T	F	S	O	S	E	L	M
P	O	A	E	E	M	O	R	A	S
S	L	R	G	I	M	F	C	B
O	G	N	I	D	W	O	R	O
R	P	S	P	L	E	H	R	U

E

TEXAS TIMES
Unions complain about migrant workers

California Herald
LOCAL BUSINESSES WELCOME MIGRANTS

Los Angeles Star
California to restrict entry of migrants

EXTRA

Work with a partner. One of you be Eddie Ingle and the other Brad Bradley.
- Make two lists, one to show the good things about migrants and the other the bad things. Rank the items in each list in order of importance.
- Display your lists on a large sheet of paper. Add a title and drawings to make it more effective.

Summary

Many Mexicans settle happily in their new surroundings but for some there can be difficulties. Migrants can be a great help to the American economy. They often provide cheap labour and work at jobs which local people are reluctant to do.

The population enquiry

As we have seen earlier in this unit, people are not spread evenly around the world. Some places are crowded whilst other places have very few people. There are many reasons for this. Some are **positive factors** which encourage people to settle in an area. Others are **negative factors** which discourage settlement. There are almost always some positive factors and some negative factors working in an area. It is the balance between the two that determines how crowded a place becomes.

Look at drawing **D** on the next page which shows an imaginary continent in the northern hemisphere. It shows many of the factors affecting population distribution that were described on pages 84 to 89. Your task in this enquiry is to determine the most likely population distribution on the continent using negative and positive factors.

How can positive and negative factors affect where people live?

1 **a)** Make a larger copy of table **B**.
   b) List the positive and negative factors for each of the areas labelled 1 to 10 on drawing **D**.
   c) For each place, decide if it is likely to be crowded, to have few people, or to be in between. Write your decision in the 'Population density' column.
   d) In the last column of the table, give reasons for your suggested population density.

2 **a)** Make a larger copy of map **C**.
   b) Show the population distribution of the continent by dividing it into areas that are likely to be crowded, have few people or be in between. Use colours similar to those on map **A** on page 84.
   c) Choose the most likely locations of three main towns and mark them on your map.
   d) Complete your map by colouring the coastline blue and giving names to the towns, mountain ranges, rivers, seas and imaginary continent.

3 Describe and suggest reasons for the locations that you have chosen for the three main towns.

A

B

Area	Positive factors	Negative factors	Population density	Reasons
1				
2				
3				
4				

C Population distribution

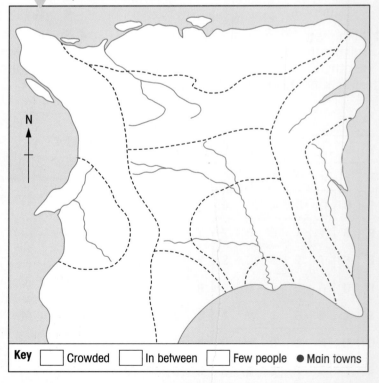

N

Key ☐ Crowded   ☐ In between   ☐ Few people   ● Main towns

D

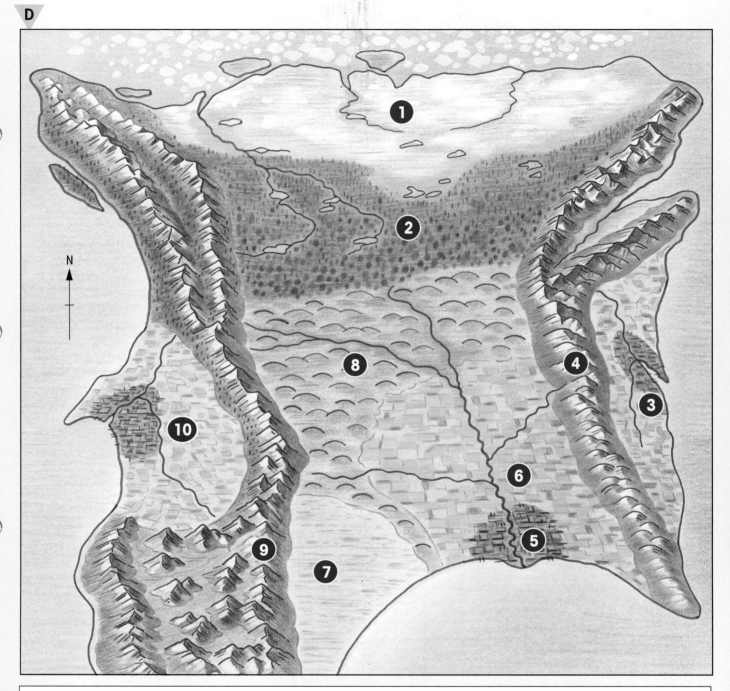

1 Mainly flat and low-lying land. Poor, thin soils. Little vegetation. Very cold.

2 Hilly with many lakes. Poor soils. Dense coniferous forest. Very cold winters.

3 Flat or gently sloping land. Raw materials available for industry. Fertile soils. Warm climate with plenty of rain.

4 Steep slopes. Thin soils. Few jobs. Poor communications.

5 Flat and low-lying land. Serves rich farming area inland. Industries and port facilities.

6 Flat or gently sloping land. Good-quality farmland. Warm summers with plenty of rain.

7 Very hot and dry. Mainly desert with few rivers. Little agriculture.

8 Mainly hilly with poor soils. Large-scale cattle farming. Few jobs. Cold winters.

9 Rugged, mountainous area. Difficult communications. Few jobs. Poor, thin soils. Wet.

10 Flat and low-lying. Fertile soils and good farming. Industries and port facilities. Good climate.

What is Kenya like?

'Jambo' means hello and is the greeting always given by Kenyans. It is usually accompanied with a broad smile and an offer of help. Indeed most Kenyans seem always to be cheerful, relaxed and willing to help others.

Yet life in Kenya can be very difficult. It is one of the poorest countries in the world, has few services, little industry and a low **standard of living**. It is called a **developing country** and is very different from the UK which is rich, has a high standard of living and is an example of a **developed country**.

Despite being poor in terms of wealth, Kenya is rich in scenery and wildlife and has become a popular tourist destination. Inland there are high mountains, volcanoes, lakes and grassy plains. On the coast there are long sandy beaches, coral reefs and tropical forest.

Most tourists are attracted by the wildlife. They go on organised tours called **safaris** and view the animals from open-topped mini-buses. After a safari, many visitors travel to the coast for a more relaxing beach holiday. Because Kenya lies on the Equator, the climate is usually hot and sunny throughout the year.

Kenya also has a varied population which is made up of people from several different groups or tribes. Each group has its own **ethnic** background with its own language, religion and way of life. Two of the best known tribes are the Maasai and the Kikuyu.

Kenya's two major cities are Nairobi, the capital, and Mombasa on the coast.

> Jambo! A developing country is usually quite poor like Kenya in Africa.

A Kenya

Key

Height in metres

▩	Over 2,000
▨	1,000–2,000
☐	500–1,000
▨	Under 500
●	Main town
—	Main road
—	Railway
Ⓑ	Photo

B

C

D

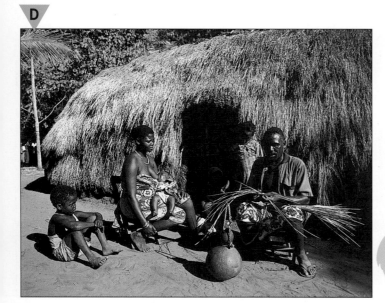

Activities

1 Give the meaning of the following terms. The Glossary at the back of the book may help you.
   a) developing country   **b)** developed country
   c) standard of living   **d)** ethnic

2 Look at map **A** opposite.
   a) Name the five countries that border Kenya.
   b) Name the four main towns in order of height above sea level. Give the highest first.
   c) How long is Kenya's coastline?
   d) How far is it by rail from Kisumu to Mombasa?
   e) What is the furthest distance from north to south?

3 Copy and complete quizword **E**, using the following clues.
   (a) Kenya's highest mountain
   (b) A line of latitude across Kenya
   (c) An ocean off Kenya's east coast
   (d) A holiday where wild animals are viewed
   (e) Kenya's main port
   (f) A traditional Kenyan greeting
   (g) A Kenyan tribe
   Make up a clue for downword (h).

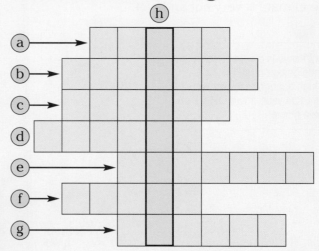

4 Imagine you are on holiday in Kenya. Use the information on this page to help you write a postcard home which describes the country.

Summary

Kenya is a developing country. Although it is not rich, it does have a wealth of spectacular scenery and wildlife.

What are Kenya's main physical features?

Most visitors to Kenya fly in to Nairobi, the country's largest city. Nairobi is in a region called the Central Highlands which millions of years ago was an area of considerable **volcanic activity**.

During that time huge cracks developed in the earth's surface. Two of the cracks ran from north to south through Kenya and as the land between the cracks collapsed, a huge **rift valley** was formed. Earth movements and volcanic eruptions are now quite rare but the cone-shaped remains of volcanoes can be seen throughout the area. Mount Kenya at 5,899 metres is the highest and best known of these.

The scenery and vegetation change dramatically towards the coast. East of the Central Highlands the land is more gently sloping and there are huge areas of grassland. A band of lush, green, tropical **rainforest** lies along the coast where the climate is very hot and wet.

A Mount Kenya

B

Mount Kenya is an old volcano. Despite being on the Equator, it is high enough to be snow-covered all year. It even has its own glacier.

The north and east of Kenya is much flatter than the centre. There is little rainfall here, so much of the land is desert with little vegetation.

The Great Rift Valley has steep sides, is very deep and in places is over 60 km wide. The valley stretches almost the whole length of Africa.

Cracks in the earth's crust

Grassland covers much of the coastal plain. The National Parks in this area are rich with wildlife.

The east coast has long sandy beaches. Coral reefs lie offshore and protect the coast. Coral thrives in the warm, clear waters of the Indian Ocean.

Kenya is on the Equator which means that average temperatures are high throughout the year. There are no winters or summers as there are in Britain. In terms of temperature, one day is very similar to the next. Seasons are defined by rainfall amounts. The rainy season is usually from April to May.

A typical day in Nairobi begins with bright, clear weather. By the afternoon clouds will have built up and there may be a shower of rain. In the evening it becomes clear and dry again, though rather cool.

Not all of Kenya is like this. The north is hot and dry and rarely has rain. Further south and along the coast there is plenty of sunshine, high temperatures throughout the year, and more rainfall. Afternoon sea-breezes cool the air on the coast but evenings are warm and very pleasant.

With attractive scenery and a climate like this, it is not surprising that Kenya's coastline has become increasingly popular with tourists.

C Climate graphs

Activities

1 a) What is the Great Rift Valley?
   b) With the help of the diagrams below, explain how the rift valley was formed.

2 Imagine that you have just taken photo **A** of Mount Kenya. Write a caption for the photo to both describe **and** explain the mountain's main features. Include the following:

• steep	• rocky	• volcano • Equator • cold
• cone-shaped	• snow-covered	• 5,899 m high

3 Look at the climate graph for Nairobi above.
   a) Which three months are the wettest?
   b) How much rainfall is there in July?
   c) What temperature would you expect in July?
   d) Why do you think Nairobi is cooler than Mombasa?

4 a) Describe the attractions for tourists to Kenya's coastline. Use the following headings:
   ● General weather   ● Coastal landforms
   ● July temperature   ● Vegetation cover
   ● July rainfall   ● Sea conditions.
   b) When is a bad time to take a holiday in the area? Give reasons for your answer.

Summary

Many of Kenya's most attractive landforms can be seen either in the Central Highlands or along the coast. Most of Kenya is hot all year but a lack of rain can be a problem.

103

Why is Kenya's population unevenly spread?

Some of the oldest known human bones have been found in Kenya.

The population of Kenya, as in most other countries, is not spread out evenly. Some places are very crowded while others have very few people living there. This is mainly due to:

- **migration** – where the people of Kenya originally came from
- **physical conditions** – differences in climate and relief in Kenya.

The movement of people into Kenya

Most present-day Kenyans are descended from African tribes who arrived in the country from three main directions (map **A**).

- Those from the north-east are fewest in number and live in the most sparsely populated area (area **W**).
- Those from the south-west are largest in number and live in the most densely populated areas (areas **X**).
- Those from the north-west live in areas which have an average population density for Kenya (area **Y**).
- Map **A** also shows that some Arabs and Indians have migrated to Kenya from the east (area **Z**). These account for only 2 per cent of the total population.

While individual tribes still remain today, their way of life has been changed through marriages with people from other ethnic groups.

Differences in physical conditions

Although Kenya is not a very large country, the physical conditions vary considerably from place to place. Map **B** shows how the distribution of population is affected by differences in rainfall, temperature, water supply, relief, soil and vegetation.

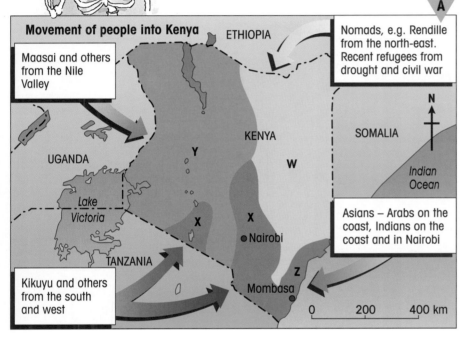

Movement of people into Kenya

Maasai and others from the Nile Valley

Nomads, e.g. Rendille from the north-east. Recent refugees from drought and civil war

Asians – Arabs on the coast, Indians on the coast and in Nairobi

Kikuyu and others from the south and west

ETHIOPIA · KENYA · SOMALIA · UGANDA · Lake Victoria · TANZANIA · Indian Ocean · Nairobi · Mombasa

0   200   400 km

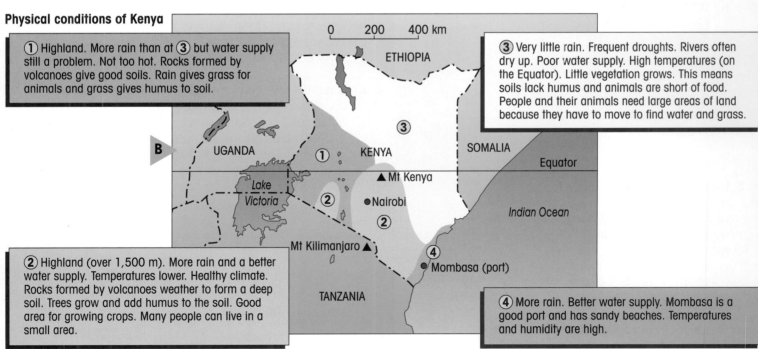

Physical conditions of Kenya

① Highland. More rain than at ③ but water supply still a problem. Not too hot. Rocks formed by volcanoes give good soils. Rain gives grass for animals and grass gives humus to soil.

③ Very little rain. Frequent droughts. Rivers often dry up. Poor water supply. High temperatures (on the Equator). Little vegetation grows. This means soils lack humus and animals are short of food. People and their animals need large areas of land because they have to move to find water and grass.

② Highland (over 1,500 m). More rain and a better water supply. Temperatures lower. Healthy climate. Rocks formed by volcanoes weather to form a deep soil. Trees grow and add humus to the soil. Good area for growing crops. Many people can live in a small area.

④ More rain. Better water supply. Mombasa is a good port and has sandy beaches. Temperatures and humidity are high.

ETHIOPIA · UGANDA · KENYA · SOMALIA · Equator · Mt Kenya · Lake Victoria · Nairobi · Mt Kilimanjaro · Mombasa (port) · TANZANIA · Indian Ocean

0   200   400 km

Present-day movements of population

In all developing countries there is a large movement of people from the countryside to the towns (see rural-to-urban migration, page 93). In Kenya it is mainly the Kikuyu who move. Their traditional home is in area ② on map **B**.

When driving through rural Kikuyu countryside it is hard to see why they want to move (photo **A**, page 110). It is one of the few parts of Kenya with roads, it has the best farmland and water supply in the country and the environment appears clean and pleasant. To those living there, especially those at school or just starting a family, it is less attractive.

Diagram **C** gives some of the reasons why many Kikuyu want to move to Nairobi, the capital of Kenya.

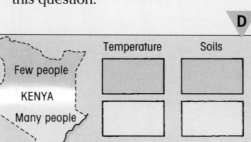

C

Nairobi has big, modern buildings which include hospitals, shops, cinemas and a university.

Kenya has one of the highest birth rates in the world. The average family size is 7.6 people. There are too many of us to find jobs on the farms and in the shambas.

The Kikuyu have lived in villages and small towns for a long time. The change to city life should be easy.

We are farmers but many of us do not own any land and if we do, the plots are very small.

We have learned some skills at school but we cannot use them in our local village.

It is not far to Nairobi so we can get work there and still visit our village.

Activities

1 Read the following statements about Kenya's population. Write out the four statements which are correct.
   - Kenya's population is spread evenly.
   - Kenya's population is not spread evenly.
   - The Maasai came from the Nile Valley and live in the south-west.
   - The Maasai came from the south-west and live in the Nile Valley.
   - The Kikuyu live in the north.
   - The Kikuyu came from the south and west and live on higher land.
   - Arabs and Indians live on the coast near Mombasa.

2 Make a copy of diagram **D** and complete it to show why the south of Kenya is more crowded than the north. For each box choose the correct word from the two given in brackets. 'Relief' has been done for you.

3 Imagine that you live in a small Kikuyu village and are about to migrate to Nairobi.
   a) Give at least three reasons for leaving your village.
   b) Give at least three advantages of living in Nairobi.
   Diagram **C** will help you to answer this question.

Summary

The distribution of population in Kenya is mainly affected by physical factors such as climate, water supply, relief and soil. Most people live in or near to the capital city of Nairobi.

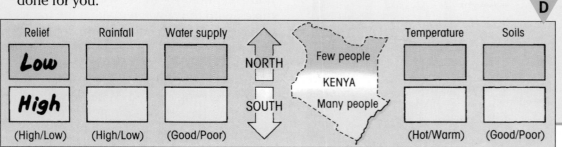

D

Relief	Rainfall	Water supply			Temperature	Soils
Low			NORTH	Few people		
High			SOUTH	Many people		
(High/Low)	(High/Low)	(Good/Poor)			(Hot/Warm)	(Good/Poor)

KENYA

What does Nairobi look like to newcomers?

Like most cities in developing countries there are two sides to Nairobi. One side is seen by overseas visitors and the relatively few wealthy Kenyans. Photo **A** shows the most important building in Nairobi. It is the Kenyatta International Conference Centre, named after Jomo Kenyatta, the first president of Kenya. Around it, in central Nairobi, are tall, modern buildings and wide, tree-lined streets.

The other side of Nairobi is the one seen by most of the Kenyans who migrate from the surrounding rural areas. Many migrants move to live with family and friends already living in Nairobi. They share houses, food and even jobs. In time the newcomers may be able to construct their own homes in one of several **shanty** settlements found on the edge of the city (photo **B**).

A

B

Living in Kibera

Kibera is one shanty settlement. It is 6 kilometres and a 7 pence bus ride from the city centre. However, most inhabitants who wish to make that journey have to walk because they cannot afford the fare.

Houses in Kibera are built close together. Sometimes it is hard to squeeze between them. The walls are usually made from mud and the roofs from corrugated iron (photos **C** and **E**). Inside there is often only one room. Very few homes have water, electricity or sewage. Julius Mwenda is a 'rich man' by Kibera standards. He has a tap and can sell water to his neighbours. He also has a toilet but this is only emptied four times a year.

Sewage runs down the tracks between the houses (photo **C**). In the wet season rain mixes with the sewage making the tracks unusable, so small children are kept indoors for several weeks. In the dry season the tracks become very dusty. Photo **D** shows an open drain along a main sidetrack being cleared. What might happen to the sewage the next time it rains?

C

Kenya has one of the highest birth rates in the world. In Kibera it is not unusual for families to have more than ten children. Very few children can read or write as there is only one small school. Many suffer from a poor diet or malaria. Others catch diseases by drinking dirty water or playing in sewage (photo **C**).

People have to find their own way to earn money. Some have small stalls from which they sell food. Others, who have learnt a skill, may turn their houses into shops (photos **B** and **E**) or collect waste material and recycle it in small workshops.

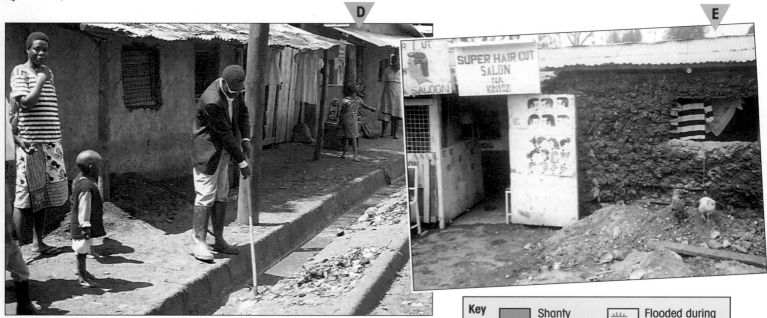

D

E

Activities

1 Give three differences between photos **A** and **B**.

2 Map **F** shows the location of shanty settlements in Nairobi.
   a) How far is Kibera from the city centre?
   b) Which direction is Kibera from the city centre?
   c) Write out the following sentence using the correct word from the pair in brackets.

'Shanty settlements are areas of (good/poor) quality housing found at the (edge/middle) of the city on (good/poor) quality building land.'

3 Using photo **C**, list four problems of life in a shanty settlement.

4 List four ways that people living in a shanty settlement can earn money.

Key — Shanty settlement — Built-up area — Flooded during rainy season

F

N

Mathare River

■ City centre

NAIROBI

Ngong River

Kibera

0   6 km

5 **a)** List four good points about living in Nairobi.
   b) Why is Nairobi described as having 'two sides'?

Summary

Cities in developing countries have two sides. Well-off people live and work in good conditions near to the city centre. Poor people often live and work in less pleasant shanty settlements a long way from the city centre.

What is the Maasai way of life?

The Maasai in Kenya

One ethnic group living in Kenya are the Maasai (see map **A** on page 104). They are **pastoralists** with herds of cattle and goats. Some are **nomadic** and have to move about to find water and grass for their animals. The Maasai depend on these animals for their daily food. It is cattle, not money, which means wealth to the Maasai. Indeed, the usual Maasai greeting is 'I hope your cows are well'.

The land where the Maasai live is fairly flat and covered with grass which depends upon the rain. The 'long rains' come between April and June, the 'short rains' in October and November. In the dry months the grass withers under the hot sun. If the rains do not come then the Maasai have to move to look for grass for their animals.

Houses

Most Maasai live in an **enkang** which is a small village made up of 20 to 50 huts (photo **A**), in which 10 to 20 families live. It is surrounded by a thick thorn hedge to keep out dangerous animals such as lions, leopards and hyenas. Tiny passages allow people and, in the evening, cattle to pass through. These passages are blocked up at night. The huts are built in a circle around an open central area. They barely reach the height of an adult Maasai (photo **B** and plan **D**) and are built from local materials.

The frame is made from wooden poles. Mud, from nearby rivers, and cow dung are used for the walls. Grass from the surrounding area is used for the roof. The hut is entered by a narrow tunnel. Apart from an opening the size of a brick, there are no windows or chimneys. The inside is dark and full of smoke from the fire. It is cool during the day, warm at night and free from flies and mosquitoes. Cowskins are laid on the floor for beds. Water and honey are stored in gourds – a ball-shaped plant with a thick skin.

A

B

C

D

Plan of the inside of a Maasai hut

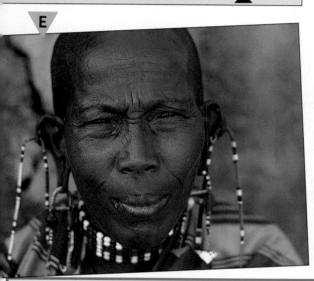

- 4 metres
- 4 metres
- Bed – hides on the floor
- Warm area for newly born cattle
- Store for water and food
- Wood store
- Open fire
- Bed – hides on the floor
- Small tunnel as entrance

E

Dress

Men wear brightly coloured 'blankets' and women wear lengths of cloth (photo **A**). The women shave their heads and wear beads around their neck, wrists and ankles. Teeth are cleaned with sticks and the men also use sticks to comb their hair. As water is often scarce, the Maasai use animal and vegetable fat to clean themselves and sweet smelling grasses for perfume.

Daily jobs

The women have to collect sticks for the fire, and water for cooking. They also make baskets and jewellery. The men spend the whole day guarding their animals. The Maasai regard the ground as sacred and believe it should not be broken. This means no crops can be grown, wells cannot be dug and, often, the dead are not buried but are left to wild animals. As crops are not grown sometimes animals are exchanged for grain.

Diet

A major part of the Maasai diet is milk mixed with blood from their cows. In times of drought only blood is used.

Activities

1 **a)** Give two facts about a developing country.
   b) What is meant by 'an ethnic group'?
   c) In which continent is Kenya?

2 **a)** Give two reasons why cattle are important to the Maasai.
   b) Write a paragraph to describe Maasai farming. Include these words: *cattle and goats, flat land, grass, rain, nomadic.*

3 Sketch **F** shows a Maasai hut and several questions. Draw the hut and add labels by answering the questions.

4 How do photo **A** and your drawing of a Maasai hut suggest that the weather is:
   a) usually warm
   b) not very wet?

F

1 What is the roof made from?

2 How wide and how long is the hut?

3 How high is the hut?

6 Why is this opening needed?

4 Describe the shape of the door

5 What are the walls made from?

Summary

Landscape, weather and wealth all affect the family life, housing, clothing and diet of the Maasai.

The Kikuyu and their environment

The largest ethnic group living in Kenya are the **Kikuyu**. Their home region is in the higher parts of the country between Mount Kenya and the capital city of Nairobi (see map **A** on page 104). Of all the ethnic groups it is the Kikuyu who have adapted most easily to western culture.

Settlement

Traditionally the Kikuyu lived in small, circular and fairly **nucleated** villages. These were similar to those of the Maasai with whom they had friendly contact. Today, driving through this part of Kenya, a visitor will see two types of settlement which have replaced these villages.

Most houses are **dispersed**. Each individual house is surrounded by a small **shamba** or garden (photo **A**). The family try to grow their yearly supply of food in the shamba. The house is circular and built from local materials. The walls are made from wooden poles tied together and the thatched roof from coconut palm leaves and grass.

Houses next to roads are often built in a **linear** pattern forming villages and small towns. Planks of wood are used for the walls and corrugated iron for the roof. The insides become very warm during the day and cold at night.

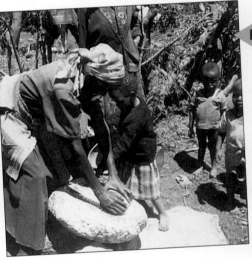

Land use and jobs

Most of the land is used for farming. The Kikuyu, unlike the Maasai, grow crops and keep very few animals. Farming is easier here because there is more rain and it is more reliable. The natural forest adds **humus** to the already deep soils. There are two types of farming in this area – **subsistence** and **commercial**.

Subsistence farming means a family grows just enough food for themselves and has very little left over to sell (photo **B**). Most shambas grow maize under the shade of small banana trees (photo **A**). Beans, yams and millet are grown as well as many tropical fruits and vegetables. No land is wasted.

Commercial farming means that crops are grown on a large scale. Early in the twentieth century the Kikuyu lands were turned into plantations by British farmers. **Plantations** are large estates, usually found in the tropics, where the natural forest is cleared and one main crop is planted in rows. In this part of Kenya the main crop is coffee on the lower slopes and tea on the higher slopes (photo **C**). Both crops need a lot of back-breaking labour and once picked are sold overseas. Today the large plantations have been broken up into smaller units and are farmed by the Kikuyu. Although they provide income for Kenya, these crops do not feed the local people.

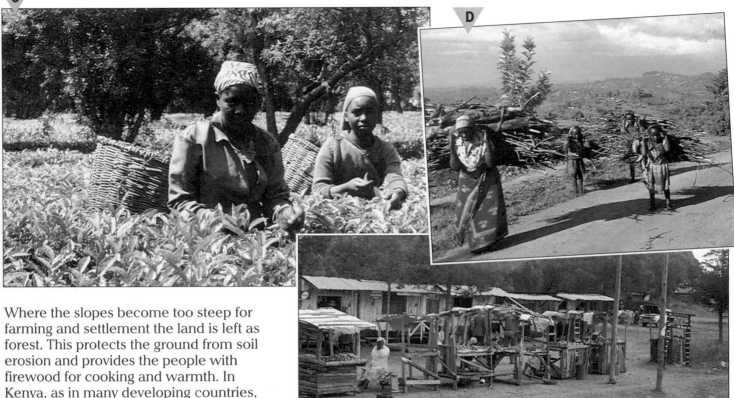

Where the slopes become too steep for farming and settlement the land is left as forest. This protects the ground from soil erosion and provides the people with firewood for cooking and warmth. In Kenya, as in many developing countries, the women have the hard job of collecting firewood (photo **D**).

The Kikuyu are well known for their crafts which they make both for themselves and

to sell in the market and in larger towns (photo **E**). The women make baskets, jewellery and clothes, and the men produce the ironwork.

Activities

1 Sketch **F** shows a Kikuyu house with its shamba or garden, and several questions. Draw the house and add labels by answering the questions.

2 Give **three** reasons why the Kikuyu find farming easier than the Maasai. Think about water supply and soils.

3 **a)** What is a plantation?
   b) Draw a star diagram to describe plantation farming in Kenya. Your diagram should try to answer the following questions:
   ● What happens to the forest?
   ● Which two crops are planted?
   ● On which type of slope is each crop planted?
   ● Where are the crops sold?
   c) Give one **advantage** and one **disadvantage** of plantation farming.

4 Apart from farming, what other jobs are done by Kikuyu men and women?

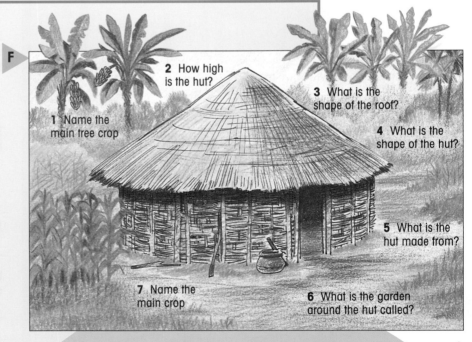

1 Name the main tree crop
2 How high is the hut?
3 What is the shape of the roof?
4 What is the shape of the hut?
5 What is the hut made from?
6 What is the garden around the hut called?
7 Name the main crop

Summary

The settlement, land use and jobs of a locality in a developing country are usually related to the environment.

Can development in Kenya be sustainable?

Kenya became an independent country in 1963. Since then it has become one of the more successful **developing countries** in East Africa. Economic growth has brought many benefits to Kenya. Some parts of the country are now developed and many Kenyans are wealthy and enjoy a high standard of living.

A

Visit
Baobab Farm
and see wildlife in their natural habitat.

* Wild animals including hippopotamus, elephant, giraffe, giant tortoise, wildebeest and zebra.
* Fish farm and crocodile hatchery.
* Reptile house with snakes and insect displays.
* Aviary with spectacular display of tropical birds.
* Guided nature trails and educational facilities.
* Information centre, shops and restaurant.

Unfortunately, progress has also brought problems both for people and the environment. Wealth has not been shared equally and the majority of Kenyans are still very poor indeed. Many living in the **shanty settlements** have an even lower standard of living than before development. As for the environment, large areas of forest have been cleared, rivers polluted, coral reefs destroyed and wildlife lost.

Some people are concerned that so-called development and progress is actually damaging Kenya. They say that development should bring about an improvement in living conditions for people. At the same time, however, it should not harm or destroy the environment nor prevent people in the future from achieving similar standards of living. Development like this is called **sustainable development.**

There are many examples in Kenya of sustainable development projects. One of these is at Baobab Farm just 10 km north of Mombasa on the coast of Kenya. The area was once a huge quarry where 25 million tonnes of coral limestone had been removed, leaving a huge, ugly scar. As photo **B** shows, the environment had been totally destroyed – there was no soil, no vegetation and no wildlife.

In 1971, the cement company that owned the quarry decided to try and restore the area to its original state. They planted quick-growing casuarina trees (photo **C**) and introduced thousands of red millipedes to break down the fallen leaves into **humus**. Earthworms, grasses and more trees were added but no chemicals were used. Within 20 years sufficient soil had formed to allow a tropical rainforest environment to develop (photo **D**).

The project is not just an environmental success. It has also become a sustainable commercial venture. Baobab Farm, as it is called, is open to school parties every morning, while in the afternoon it attracts other visitors. It is now one of Kenya's most visited tourist attractions.

B Bamburi limestone quarry

Before

C Casuarina trees planted

During

D Baobab Farm restored environment

After

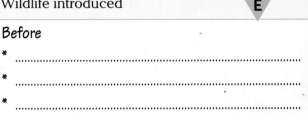

Activities

1 Complete these three sentences:
   a) Sustainable development is ...
   b) Sustainable development should ...
   c) Sustainable development should not ...

2 Look at the following list of statements about the restoration scheme at Baobab Farm. Copy and complete diagram **E** by putting each statement into the correct box.
   * Casuarina trees planted
   * Tropical rainforest returns
   * Tourist facility opened
   * Limestone quarried
   * Red millipedes introduced
   * Bare, ugly landscape
   * New soil develops
   * No soil, vegetation or wildlife
   * Wildlife introduced

E

Before
* ....
* ....
* ....

↓

During
* ....
* ....
* ....

↓

After
* ....
* ....
* ....

3 Draw a star diagram to show the main attractions of Baobab Farm

4 What features of Baobab Farm make it a good example of sustainable development?

Summary

Sustainable development should improve people's quality of life and standard of living without wasting resources or destroying the environment. Kenya's Baobab Farm is an example of successful sustainable development.

What is a developing country?

By now you should be aware of many differences between living in Kenya and in your home region in the UK. These differences include ethnic groups, dress, housing, jobs, wealth and the quality of life. Kenya is an example of a **developing country**. What is a developing country? How is life in a developing country different from life in a developed country like the UK?

In the UK most, but not all, people earn a lot of money compared with those in a developing country. They live in good houses, have their own cars and videos and can afford good food and holidays. Compared with Kenya most people in Britain have a high **standard of living**. Kenya is considered to be 'poor' and the UK to be 'rich'. Most people see the difference in wealth as the main difference between a developing country and a developed country.

The wealth of a country is given by its **gross national product** (**GNP**). This is the total amount of money made by a country from its raw materials, its manufactured goods and its services.

Notice that GNP is always given in American dollars (US$). The total amount can then be divided by the total number of people living in that country. This gives the average amount of money available for every person living in the country.

By giving the GNP in US$ it is easy to compare different countries. Table **A** gives the average income (GNP) per person for five developing countries and three developed countries.

Apart from wealth there are many other ways of trying to measure the level of a country's development (table **B**).

A

	Country	GNP (US$ per person)
Developing countries	Bangladesh	240
	Brazil	3,640
	Egypt	790
	Kenya	270
	Peru	2,310
Developed countries	Japan	39,640
	UK	18,913
	USA	26,980

B

Jobs	Primary activities give most jobs in a developing country. A developed country has fewer primary activities and more secondary and service jobs.
Trade	A developing country usually has to sell raw materials at a low price and has to buy manufactured goods from developed countries at a high price.
Population	A developing country has a higher **birth** and **death rate** (page 90), more young children dying (high **infant mortality**), adults dying at a younger age (short **life expectancy**) and a faster population increase than a developed country.
Health	A developing country has less money to spend on training doctors and nurses and in providing hospitals and medicines.
Education	The large number of children and lack of money for schools in a developing country mean fewer people can read and write than in a developed country (low **literacy rate**).

The 'rich' North and the 'poor' South

What happens when the different methods used in table **B** to measure the level of development of a country are put together? The result is a group of mainly 'rich' countries which are found in the North and a group of mainly 'poor' countries which lie to the South. Map **C** shows this division.

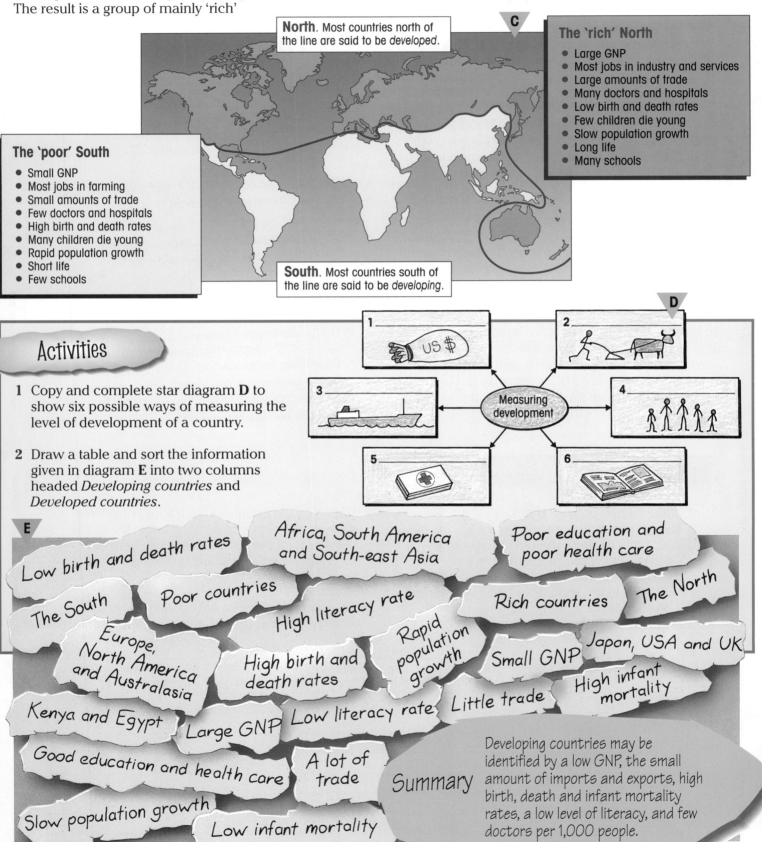

North. Most countries north of the line are said to be *developed*.

C

The 'rich' North

- Large GNP
- Most jobs in industry and services
- Large amounts of trade
- Many doctors and hospitals
- Low birth and death rates
- Few children die young
- Slow population growth
- Long life
- Many schools

The 'poor' South

- Small GNP
- Most jobs in farming
- Small amounts of trade
- Few doctors and hospitals
- High birth and death rates
- Many children die young
- Rapid population growth
- Short life
- Few schools

South. Most countries south of the line are said to be *developing*.

D

1. US $
2.
3.
Measuring development
4.
5.
6.

Activities

1 Copy and complete star diagram **D** to show six possible ways of measuring the level of development of a country.

2 Draw a table and sort the information given in diagram **E** into two columns headed *Developing countries* and *Developed countries*.

E

Low birth and death rates

Africa, South America and South-east Asia

Poor education and poor health care

The South

Poor countries

High literacy rate

Rich countries

The North

Europe, North America and Australasia

High birth and death rates

Rapid population growth

Small GNP

Japan, USA and UK

Kenya and Egypt

Large GNP

Low literacy rate

Little trade

High infant mortality

Good education and health care

A lot of trade

Slow population growth

Low infant mortality

Summary Developing countries may be identified by a low GNP, the small amount of imports and exports, high birth, death and infant mortality rates, a low level of literacy, and few doctors per 1,000 people.

The Kenya enquiry

We have already seen that all countries are different. Some are rich and have high standards of living whilst others are poor and have low standards of living. Countries that differ in this way are said to be at different stages of development.

In this unit you have learned much about Kenya. You will certainly know by now that Kenya is very different from the UK and also, certainly in terms of wealth, that it is very poor. Indeed Kenya is an almost perfect example of a **developing country**.

As we have seen, however, measuring development can be difficult. Development, after all, is about quality of life. Some countries may be economically poor, but their people can still be cheerful, relaxed and generally happy with their lives.

In this enquiry you work for a department of the British Government responsible for overseas development and have been asked to make a report on Kenya's level of development. The report will be in four parts, as shown in drawing **A**. Pages 114 and 115 of this book will be helpful to you.

A ▶

British Overseas Aid

The Kenya Report

1 How developed is Kenya compared with the UK?

2 How developed is Kenya compared with neighbouring countries in Africa?

3 How developed is Kenya in terms of social and cultural measures of development?

4 In which areas of development (as shown in table **B**) is Kenya in greatest need of improvement? What might be done to help the country make progress?

In each case suggest reasons for your answer. You should consider economic, social and cultural factors.

* **Economic factors** are about the wealth of a country.
* **Social factors** are concerned with standards of living and quality of life.
* **Cultural factors** are about traditions and the way of life.

How developed is Kenya?

1 a) Make a copy of table **B** below.
  b) Using information from diagram **C**, complete your table to show the rank order of the seven countries for each measure of development. The most developed will score 1 and the least developed will score 7.
  c) Add the scores together for each country, and complete the Total column.

2 Write out the countries from your completed table as a 'League table of development'. The country with the lowest score will be most developed and should be at the top of the league.

3 Complete the report using your answer to Activity 1 and information in diagrams **C** and **D**.

B ▶

Country	Wealth (highest first)	Trade (highest first)	Life expectancy (highest first)	People/doctor (lowest first)	Literacy rate (highest first)	TOTAL
UK						
Ethiopia						
Kenya						
Somali Rep.						
Sudan						
Tanzania						
Uganda						

C

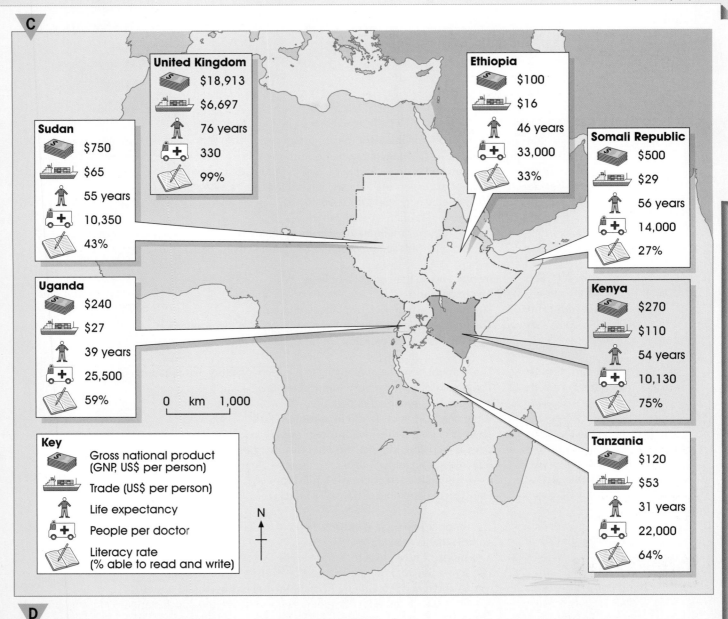

United Kingdom
- 💵 $18,913
- 🚢 $6,697
- 🧍 76 years
- 🚑 330
- 📖 99%

Ethiopia
- 💵 $100
- 🚢 $16
- 🧍 46 years
- 🚑 33,000
- 📖 33%

Sudan
- 💵 $750
- 🚢 $65
- 🧍 55 years
- 🚑 10,350
- 📖 43%

Somali Republic
- 💵 $500
- 🚢 $29
- 🧍 56 years
- 🚑 14,000
- 📖 27%

Uganda
- 💵 $240
- 🚢 $27
- 🧍 39 years
- 🚑 25,500
- 📖 59%

Kenya
- 💵 $270
- 🚢 $110
- 🧍 54 years
- 🚑 10,130
- 📖 75%

Tanzania
- 💵 $120
- 🚢 $53
- 🧍 31 years
- 🚑 22,000
- 📖 64%

0   km   1,000

Key
- 💵 Gross national product (GNP, US$ per person)
- 🚢 Trade (US$ per person)
- 🧍 Life expectancy
- 🚑 People per doctor
- 📖 Literacy rate (% able to read and write)

N

D

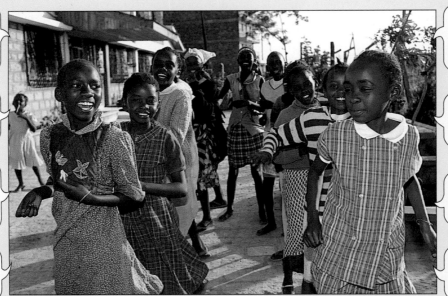

Our country is making progress but most of us are still very poor.

We have a wealth of beautiful scenery and exciting wildlife.

Family values are important to us and we are always willing to help others.

We still need a clean, reliable water supply and more food.

Kenyan children always seem to have a smile on their faces and be full of fun.

Our traditional way of life is interesting and colourful.

We have some of the best athletes in the world.

People in Kenya are well known for being cheerful and friendly.

Glossary

A

Acid rain	Rainwater containing chemicals which come from burning fossil fuels. *78*
Agribusiness	Large-scale farming that uses modern scientific methods. *31*
Agriculture	The growing of crops and rearing of animals. *28*
Alluvium	Sometimes called silt. Fine soil left behind after a river floods. *13*
Arable farming	The growing of crops. *28, 29, 30, 31, 40*
Arch	An opening through a rock. *14*
Assembling	Putting together manufactured parts to make things such as computers or cars. *44, 52, 53*
Attractive countryside	Areas of pleasant scenery such as mountains, rivers, lakes and coasts. *68*

B

Bay	A wide curved inlet of a sea or lake. *14*
Beach	An area of sand or pebbles along a coast. *15*
Biological weathering	The breakdown of rock by plants and animals. *5*
Birth rate	The number of people being born each 1,000 of the population. *90, 107, 114*
Business parks	New offices built in pleasant surroundings on the edge of cities. *56, 57*

C

Capital	The amount of money belonging to a country, factory or a person. *108*
Chemical weathering	The breakdown of rock by chemical action. *5*
Clean-up	A method of getting rid of pollution. *17, 19*
Commercial farming	When farm produce is sold for a profit. *110*
Conservation	The protection of the environment. *66*
Conservationists	People who care for and look after the environment. *68, 71, 79*
Construction industry	Building and repairing places, e.g. houses, factories and roads. *44*
Cross-section	A view at right-angles across a landform. *12*
Current	The flow of water in a certain direction. *6*

D

Death rate	The number of people dying per 1,000 of the population. *90, 114*
Densely populated	An area that is crowed. *84, 87, 104*
Density	A measure of how close together people live in an area. *84*
Deposition	The laying down of material carried by rivers, sea, ice or wind. *7*
Deposition landforms	Landscape features made up of material that has been laid down. *15*
Developed country	A country which has a lot of money, many services and a high standard of living. *100, 108, 114, 115*
Developing country	A country which is often quite poor, has few services and a low standard of living. *100, 108, 112, 114, 115, 116*

E

Economic activity	A primary, secondary or tertiary industry. *24*
Endangered species	Wildlife in danger of becoming extinct. *70*
Energy	The power to do something and to give off heat. *46, 74*
Environment	The natural or physical surroundings where people, plants and animals live. *Unit 4*
Erosion	The wearing away and removal of rock, soil, etc. by rivers, sea, ice and wind. *4, 6, 7*
Erosion landforms	Landscape features resulting from the wearing away of rock. *14*
Ethnic	A group of people with common characteristics of race, nationality, language, religion or culture. *100, 101*
Exploitation	The selfish use or development of something for our own benefit, without considering how it will affect other people and the environment. *76*
Extinct	Wildlife which can no longer be found living on earth. *70*

F

Factories	Places where things are made from natural resources and raw materials. *Unit 3*
Farm woodland scheme	Money given to farmers to plant trees instead of crops. *35*
Flood plain	The flat area at the bottom of a valley which is often flooded. *13*
Food mountains and lakes	Surplus supplies of farm products. *35*
Fossil fuels	Fuels from the remains of plants or ancient life. *74, 78*

	Frost shattering	A form of weathering where water in cracks freezes and expands to split or shatter the rock. *4*
G	**Global warming**	The warming of the earth's atmosphere by burning fossil fuels and releasing carbon dioxide. *78*
	Gorge	A steep-sided valley. *10, 21, 23*
	Greenfield sites	Land found on the edge of an urban area which has not yet been built on. *56*
	Gross national product (GNP)	The wealth of a country. Its total income divided by its total population. *114, 115, 117*
H	**Headland**	A part of the coastline that juts out into the sea and usually ends in a cliff. *14*
	Hedgerows	Bushes and small trees that are used as field boundaries. *36, 68*
	High-tech industries	Industries using advanced machines and skilled people, e.g. computers and electronics. *56-59*
	Historic sites	Important old settlements and buildings which are interesting to people. *68*
	Humus	The remains of plants and animals left in the soil. *112*
I	**Industrialised**	Using machines and power (energy) to make things. *48*
	Infant mortality rate	The number of children out of every 1,000 born alive that die before they reach the age of one year. *114*
	International migration	The movement of people from one country to another. *93*
	Irrigated	Land that has been artificially watered. *30*
J	**Just-in-time**	A system used in car making where components are supplied to the assembly-line just hours before they are needed. *53*
L	**Labour**	Workers. Employed people. *46*
	Landscape	The scenery. What the land looks like. *4*
	Life expectancy	The average number of years a person can expect to live. *114, 116, 117*
	Literacy rate	The number of people who can read and write. *114, 116, 117*
	Load	The material carried by a river. *9*
M	**Market**	A place where raw materials and goods are sold. A group of people who buy raw materials or goods. *46, 49, 52*
	Meander	A large bend in a river. *13*
	Migrant workers	People who live in one country and travel each day to work in another. *94*
	Migration	The movement of people from one place to another to live or to work. *92, 93, 94, 96, 104, 106*
	Mining	The extraction of minerals from deep under the ground, e.g. coal, iron ore. *24, 25*
	Mixed farming	The growing of crops and rearing of animals on the same farm. *28, 29*
N	**Natural increase**	The difference between birth and death rates. *91*
	Natural resources	Raw materials which are obtained from the environment, e.g. water, coal, soil. *24, 45*
	Negative factors	Things that discourage people from living in a place. *86, 87, 98*
	Non-renewable resources	Resources that can only be used once, e.g. coal, oil. *74, 78*
O	**Onion-skin weathering**	The breakdown of rock by heating and cooling which cause the surface layers to peel off. *4*
P	**Pastoral farming**	The rearing of animals. *28, 29*
	Pastoralists	Farmers who look after herds of animals. *108*
	Plantation	Large farmed area often of one crop which is sold for cash. *110*
	Plunge pool	A hollow at the base of a waterfall caused by erosion. *10, 23*
	Polar regions	Cold areas of the world near to the North and South Poles. *88*
	Pollution	Noise, dirt and other harmful substances produced by people and machines which spoil an area. *16, 60, 61, 66, 67, 79*
	Population distribution	How many people are spread out over an area. *84, 86, 98, 104*
	Population explosion	A sudden rapid rise in the number of people. *90*
	Population growth	The increase in the number of people in an area. *90*
	Population growth rate	A measure of how quickly the number of people in an area increases. *90*
	Positive factors	Things that encourage people to live in an area. *86, 87, 98*
	Power	Energy needed to work machines and to produce electricity. *46*

	Primary activity	Collecting and using natural resources, e.g. farming, fishing, forestry and mining. *Unit 2, 44, 45, 114*
	Pull factors	Things that attract people to live in an area. *93*
	Push factors	Things that make people want to leave an area. *93*
Q	**Quarry**	Where rock is cut from the surface of the land. *24, 25, 26, 27, 79*
R	**Rainforest**	Tall, dense forest found in hot, wet climates. *102*
	Raw materials	Natural resources which are used to make things. *24, 46, 48, 53, 67*
	Recycling	Turning waste into something which is usable again. *74*
	Redevelop	To knock everything down and start all over again. *54, 74, 75*
	Renewable resources	Resources which can be used over and over again. *74, 75*
	Resources	Things which can be useful to people. They may be natural like coal and iron ore, or of other value like money and skilled workers. *60, 67*
	Rift valley	A steep-sided valley formed by the sinking of land between two faults or cracks. *102, 103*
	River cliff	The steep slope cut into the valley side by erosion on the outside of a river bend. *12*
	Rural-to-urban migration	The movement of people from the countryside to the towns and cities. *93, 105*
S	**Science park**	An estate of high-tech industries having links with a university. *56, 57*
	Seasonal jobs	Employment that lasts for only part of the year. *94*
	Secondary activities	Where natural resources are turned into goods which we can use. *Unit 3, 114*
	Service industry	See Tertiary industry
	Set-aside land	Scheme where farmers are paid for not farming their land. *35*
	Sewage	Waste material from homes and industry. *16, 17, 106*
	Shanty settlement	A collection of shacks and poor-quality housing which often lack electricity, a water supply and sewage disposal. *106, 112*
	Silt	Sometimes called alluvium. Fine soil left behind after a river floods. *13*
	Site	The place where a settlement or a factory is located. *46, 50*
	Soil erosion	The removal of soil by wind or water. *37*
	Sparsely populated	An area that has few people living in it. *84, 87, 104*
	Spit	A long narrow tongue of sand and shingle which grows out from the shoreline. *15*
	Spoil tip	Piles of waste material left after mining and quarrying. *25, 26*
	Stack	A pillar of rock on a sea coast separated from the mainland by erosion. *14*
	Standard of living	How well-off a person or a country is. *94, 100, 114*
	Subsidies	Money paid to farmers by the government or European Union. They usually come in the form of grants and loans. *31, 33*
	Subsistence	Growing just enough food for your own needs with nothing left over to sell. *110*
	Sustainable development	A method of progress that does not waste resources and looks after the needs of today without damaging resources for the future. *112, 113*
T	**Technology**	New ways of using resources and developing new equipment. *80*
	Temporary migrants	People who live and work in a country for a short time before returning home. *94*
	Tertiary industry	An industry that provides a service for people. Teachers and shop assistants are in this type of industry. *44, 45*
	Thermal power	Electricity produced by burning fossil fuels. *78*
	Trade	The movement of goods and services between countries. *114*
	Transport	Ways of moving people and goods from one place to another. *46, 51, 80*
	Transportation	The movement of eroded material by rivers, sea, ice and wind. *7*
V	**V-shaped valley**	A valley which has been eroded by a river so that its shape from one side to the other looks like a letter V. *8, 9*
W	**Waterfall**	A sudden fall of water over a steep drop. *10, 94, 95, 96*
	Weathering	The action of the weather, plants and animals on rocks. The rocks are broken down without being removed. *4, 6, 8*
	Wetlands	Marshy areas which are a habitat for wildlife. *36, 68*
	Wilderness	A place which has not been developed by people and is still in its natural state. *72*
	Wildlife habitats	The homes of plant and animals. *38, 68, 76*